CW00566545

Miniature pigs

Miniature pigs as ̗

Mini Pigs book for housing, keeping, diet, health, costs, pros and cons.

By

Olivia Harper

Table of Contents

Introduction

I want to thank you and congratulate you for buying the book 'Micro pigs as pets'. This book will help you to understand everything you need to know about domesticating a micro pig. You will learn all the aspects related to raising the micro pig successfully at home. You will be able to understand the pros and cons, behaviour, basic care, keeping, housing, diet and health related to the animal.

There are people who are impressed by the adorable looks of the micro pig. They think that this reason is enough to domesticate the animal, but domestication of a micro pig has its unique challenges and issues.

If you are not ready for these challenges, then you are not ready to domesticate the animal. If you have already bought or adopted a micro pig, even then you need to understand your pet so that you can take care of him in a better way. It is important that you understand that owning any pet will have its advantages and disadvantages.

Please note that, although there are female micro pigs, we shall refer to them as "he" for ease.

You should see whether with all its pros and cons, the animal fits well into your household. Domesticating and taming a pet is not only fun. There is a lot of hard work that goes into it. It is important that you are ready to commit before you decide to domesticate the animal. If you are a prospective buyer, then understanding these points will help you to make a wise decision.

When you bring a pet home, it becomes your responsibility to raise the pet in the best way possible. You have to provide physically, mentally, emotionally and financially for the pet. Before you embark on this journey of raising your pet, it is important to evaluate your resources and make sure that you are ready for the pet. You should also evaluate the practical side of things. It is important that you know that the cost of bringing up a micro pig might be more than the cost you would have to encounter while raising a dog or a cat.

It is important to have a thorough understanding about the animal. Spend some time to learn everything about the micro pig. This will help you know your pet better. The more you know about your pet, the better bond you will form with him. Whenever you get a pet home, you have to make sure that you are all ready for the responsibilities ahead. A pet is like a family member. This is the basic requirement to domesticate an animal. It is more than important that you take care of all the responsibilities for the animal.

If you wish to raise a micro pig as a pet, there are many things that you need to keep in mind. It can get very daunting for a new owner. Because of the lack of information, you will find yourself getting confused as to what should be done and what should be avoided.

It is important that you understand the basic behaviour of the micro pig. This will help you to understand what lies ahead of you. If you understand how a micro pig should be cared for, you will make it work for you. You should aim at learning about the animal and then doing the right thing for him. This will help you to form a relationship with him.

Once you form a relationship with the micro pig, it gets better and easier for you as the owner. The pet will grow up to be friendly and adorable. He will also value the bond as much as you do. This will be good for the pet and also for you as the pet owner in the long run.

If you are in two minds about whether you need a micro pig or not, then this book will make it simpler for you. You should objectively look at the various advantages and disadvantages of owning a micro pig. This will help you to make your decision.

This book is meant to equip you with all the knowledge that you need to have before buying the micro pig and bringing it home. This book will help you understand the basic behaviour and antics of the animal. You will also learn various tricks and tips. These tips and tricks will be a quick guide when you are looking for different ways to have fun with your pet. It is important that a prospective buyer has all the important information regarding a micro pig.

Chapter 1: Understanding a micro pig

For most people, the concept of a miniature pig or miniature livestock itself may seem quite different. It is almost as if they aren't the real deal.

Usually, the first question that comes up is why anyone would want a miniature pig. Then, the second concern is if these are regular sized pigs with some genetic or developmental defects. To learn more about these two common queries we will have to take a peek into the history of livestock and their association with people.

1. What is a miniature pig or micro pig?

If you are looking to domesticate this unique animal then it is critical that you make an effort to understand what a miniature pig is. A breed of pigs that is much smaller in size and weight compared to the usual pigs is known as miniature pigs. They are also called as micro pigs.

It should be noted here that there are many breeds of miniature pigs, such as Potbellied and Kunekune. There are many other breeds of micro pigs that are derived from cross breeding between the available and popular breeds.

2. What is the difference between the micro pig and a normal sized pig?

Many a times, prospective owners wonder whether the only difference between the micro pig and the large sized pigs is the size of the animals. It should be noted here that there are many other features that can help distinguish a micro and other pigs.

The ears of the miniature pig are very small in size. These ears are perked back in their appearance. The back of the pig is known to be swayed in appearance.

Most micro pigs are said to have pot-bellies. This is what makes them stand out in comparison to other pigs that are normal sized.

The entire look of the pig is very chubby if you care to look carefully. The pig has a compact body and curved profile, and its legs are short and rounded.

3. A brief history

Modern livestock can be traced back to almost six thousand years using the archaeological evidence. Two species, namely the *Bos taurus* or the hump-less livestock or the *Bos indicus* or the humped livestock are believed to be the predecessors of the modern domesticated livestock. These two species were generated by another species, which is classified as *Bos primigenius.*

It has been noticed that these livestock gradually reduced in size because of inadequate feeding. It is also believed that they were downsized deliberately to be able to handle them and house them properly. The recent findings revealed several remains of livestock that were not only less bulky but also smaller in size.

Around the 19th century, certain breeds that hailed from the British Iles such as the Kerrys were prized for their small stature and were chosen as decorations in county estates. They also gained popularity because of their ability to mow the lawns naturally.

In Northern Europe, it was the norm to have a family pig or a small-sized herd. They were raised to provide meat and also to help in cultivation.

In the tropical regions, a family pig is still a common occurrence, with preference given to the smaller breeds such as the Zebu livestock.

Post the Second World War, demand for better quality meat increased. In addition to that, resources for better nutrition, breeding and feeding also became available. With an increase in production capabilities, the mindset shifted towards "the bigger the better".

This move was supported by producers, as it would increase their profits tremendously. Livestock that had longer legs and more height were easier to herd as they would lose less weight and feel less stressed even when moved across large ranges.

With these developments and with better facilities of transport and refrigeration, larger pigs began to gain popularity. While the whole world was shifting towards large sized livestock, there were some who were still researching about the smaller breeds and methods to produce healthy specimens of these breeds.

In the late 1960s, breeding smaller livestock was started by a Mexican rancher. He admitted that he wanted to create miniature livestock as a pet for those who could afford it. He then partnered with a veterinary researcher and shifted the focus of the project towards producing more on a smaller piece of land. This drew the interest of several organizations across the world, the most noteworthy being the US National Research Council.

Then, a Texas breeder noticed that the size of the pigs and livestock on the show ring was steadily on the rise. So, he decided to start a program to downsize the Hereford Livestock in the 1970s. This breed hails from Herefordshire in England. The goal of this breeder was to produce specimens that were smaller in size but excellent in their conformation.

Simultaneously, a research project was being conducted in Australia. This project, which went on from 1974 to 1993, was primarily focused on determining if the smaller specimens of livestock were more efficient in producing meat. This led to the production of the Lowline breed. This breed was used as the closed herd of small sized livestock in this project. The efficiency was the same as the larger pigs and thus the interest in this breed continued, allowing them to survive.

In Seattle, Washington, around the same time, breeders Arlene Gradwohl and Richard Gradwohl noticed that urbanization was happening quickly. There were several housing developments that began to mushroom around the area. Being a farm man himself, Richard wanted to make sure that he was able to retain the rural lifestyle. He had a background as a business professor and he began to research about the commercial value of the possible opportunities to maintain a farm life.

He realized that smaller livestock had greater value on smaller property. Since he advocated innovation, he began his research on miniature livestock and learnt line-breeding techniques. He got extremely interested in developing new breeds of these miniature pigs. He has developed almost 18 new breeds of miniature livestock until now.

It is true that third world countries and other developing nations still maintain interest in the larger breeds, but several farm owners have realized that it is futile to pursue larger livestock. In fact, during the 1980', research conducted by the National Research Council helped raise awareness in almost 80 countries about the potential of miniature livestock. This, they claimed, would actually help develop these nations.

In the United States, there have been significant changes in farming. The amount of land available has reduced and several hobby farms and small acreages have gained popularity. A census of agriculture in 2002 revealed that there has been an increase in small farms by 46% since 1979. There have also been several changes in farm ownerships, giving rise to new typology groups such as retirement farms and lifestyle farms. Today, most farm operators are the sole owners as well.

There are tax incentives for small-scale farmers. They can get benefits by showing any use of land for agricultural purposes. For many, farming is a way of life post retirement, some own small farms for ecological reasons, natural living reasons and also the desire to lead a simple farm life. This is one of the significant reasons for growing interest in miniature livestock.

4. Life span of miniature pigs

A potbellied pig, which is the first choice as the miniature pet pig, has a life span of 12-18 years. The teacup piglets have a life span of over five years.

It is known that a pig that is cared for and groomed in a good way will have a good life span. The key is to provide them with the right environment and also the right nutrition. This will help them to grow, stay healthy and live longer.

5. Body structure

All the breeds of the miniature pigs are very small in size. In fact, some of the breeds are smaller than the rest of them.

The head is round in shape. The head and eyes are bigger in comparison to the body. The ears have a peculiar shape and are swayed back. The structure of the ears helps the pig to protect itself from many bacteria and infections.

The legs, snout and the neck are very short for the micro pig. If you notice the tail, it is also very short. The end of the tail will have some hair on it.

6. Size and weight

It should be noted that there is not one specific number that can define the size and weight of micro pigs.

As discussed, the micro pigs have many breeds. These breeds can vary from one another in terms of the actual size and weight. It is known that most breeds of the miniature pig come under the range of 75 pounds/34 kilograms to 200 pounds/91 kilograms. If you see the numbers, you will realize that the micro pigs are quite heavy.

On average, a fully-grown micro pig will be around 15 inches in height and 40 kilograms in weight.

To get a clearer idea, you can compare the size and weight with a pet dog that you might have. The micro pig would be on a heavier side when seen in terms of weight. So, if you can't handle a Labrador well, you might find it very difficult to handle a micro pig. Important to note here that not all micro pigs will grow to the size of a Labrador: some micro pigs might stay smaller whilst others might get bigger.

The most important message here is to be prepared for your micro pig to become bigger than you first expected. Most of them certainly don't stay the cute tiny piggies you often see online or on TV.

These standards show us that miniature livestock start of really small. The weight of the livestock varies from one breed to another. The standards are an average measurement to determine if a specimen is healthy or not. If you are solely into hobby breeding and farming, a few inches of deviation from standards will not matter.

However, in the case of miniature livestock shows, it is imperative to stick to the standards that have been established for specific breeds in order to qualify to showcase your livestock.

7. Breeds of the Miniature pig

As mentioned before, several breeds of miniature livestock have been developed over the years. Each breed has its own utilitarian value and there are reasons why some people prefer a certain breed.

There are a few breeds that have specific guidelines. You can find official clubs dedicated to each of these breeds such as the American Pig Association who have websites that list all necessary characteristics. Some of the breeds are as follows:

- Pot bellied pigs: These are the most popular breed of miniature pigs. The pigs attain a height of 12-14 and weigh over 200 pounds. They are also called teacup pot bellies. The authorities on the standardization of this breed are the American Dexter Livestock Association and the Purebred Dexter Livestock Association of North America.

- Juliani pigs: The pigs attain a height of 15-18 and weigh over 50 pounds. These breeds were bred to be the original small area livestock from Ireland. They serve a dual purpose. They come in many colors including red, dun and black.

- Kunekune: They are smaller in comparison to other breeds. They are plump in appearance and have round legs. These livestock have always been smaller in size, which has made them popular in breeding programs in order to create smaller varieties of other breeds.

- Ossabawa island pigs: The authorities on standardization of this breed are The Miniature Breeders Association and the Miniature Clun. You can register your pig or piglet with the association. These miniatures are red in color with white faces just like the full sized ones.

- African pygmy or guinea hog: They were included in the National Western Stock show for the first time in the year 2000. A steady increase in numbers was noticed not just in the United States but in Canada as well. The pigs attain a weight over 300 pounds.

- Mexican hairless pig: The pigs attain a height of 16-24 and weigh over 200 pounds. This breed is also a popular choice for breeding programs that create smaller versions of livestock breed. This breed is known for being extremely resistant to heat and diseases.

- Choctaw hogs: These longhaired pigs and piglets are known for their distinct appearance. Although there are no exact records of how diverse the range of this breed is, they have become quite popular. The hardiness, the grazing brush and the thick hide of this breed is the reason for their popularity.

- Other breeds: There are many miniature livestock breeds that are being developed on a regular basis with a lot of support from enthusiasts. They are lower in numbers but have had a lot of mention in research and also in livestock shows.

Today, the International Miniature Livestock Breeders Society lists about 28 species of miniature breeds. Because of constant work from breeders like the Gradwohls, there are new ones that are mushrooming in different areas.

You can visit the website of the IMCBS for more information on the right methods of producing miniature breeds to earn a good profit. There are also details on trademarking a new breed developed by you.

There are several reasons why new breeds are developed. Some of them want specific physical traits to create smaller varieties for the pet market in general. The IMCBS also tells you in detail how the registered breeds were developed so you can get an idea. The possibilities are limitless as long as breeders are genuine and work under the guidelines provided to make sure that the livestock produced is healthy and utilitarian.

8. Why choose miniature livestock?

The best thing about miniature livestock is that they have the same qualities as their large sized counterparts. They are also more convenient to manage in an urban set up. That is why several farm owners are switching to miniature livestock. Some of the best reasons to own miniature livestock are:

They don't need much space

In the case of full sized livestock, you need five acres for two. In the case of miniature livestock you can have two per acre of land. This depends on the grass available and the supplements that you provide with the feed.

Livestock do well when raised in herds. It is possible to have one or more herds even on a smaller property when you raise miniature livestock.

Gentler personality

In comparison to their larger counterparts, miniature livestock tend to be more docile. Since they are small in size and easy to manage, their owners work directly with them from birth. That makes it possible to halter train them at a very young age. It is also much easier to control miniature livestock should they get out of hand.

The fact that they are easier to handle makes them a better choice for those who have retired. With large livestock, it can be a little intimidating, especially if you have kids at home.

Return on investment

Miniature livestock can be pricey. In order to get started, you will have to make a big investment. It depends on the rarity of the breed, the availability and the breeding heritage.

In some cases, breeds that have been developed with specific traits and qualities can cost tens of thousands of dollars. However, when you enter your livestock into breeding programs, you may be able to create more than one specimen of your breed or may be lucky enough to develop new species altogether. Either way, you will be able to get guaranteed returns on your investments with miniature livestock.

Varied uses

One of the most important reasons for the increased popularity of smaller livestock is their value on farms and for commercial purposes. They have in fact proved to be a lot more efficient in terms of pork production, breeding and also as show livestock.

Of course, they also make great pets besides being very useful commercially. They have a very friendly nature that also makes them perfect for petting zoos and to educate more people through agri-tourism.

Selling miniature livestock or using them for the same can be good business. The population of miniatures is still low in comparison to the regular sized ones but the demand increases by almost 20% per annum.

There are requirements that include a good record about the heritage of the livestock, documentation of their size when they are born, the immunization records and also the ease of calving. You can sell the breeding samples of your miniature livestock for a good price. Per straw of breeding sample can earn you between $50-100/£10-50. You can sell embryos of as high as $1500/£700.

Of course pork production is an important use. Today healthy, and hormone free meat is in demand and that makes miniature livestock a good option for farm owners. Meat production is, of course, one of the biggest income generators for farm owners. There are certain breeds that provide both and have, therefore, become popular.

You do not have to worry about quantity either. With breeds like the miniature Kunekune, you don't have to compromise on the butterfat content and the protein content. If you are raising miniature livestock as pets, this can become a source of meat for your family.

Miniature breeds are eligible for several national and state level livestock shows, which have attractive cash prizes. The sheer interest in miniature livestock and the curiosity about them has become a USP, promoting their use in livestock shows. The respective clubs for miniature livestock have also started special shows in various categories such as pre- junior categories for younger piglets and pigs.

Of course, they are increasingly becoming popular as house pets. While this is still a new practice, several farms and breeders have reported an increase in sales solely to keep miniature livestock as pets. Keeping a miniature pig as a pet comes with several benefits. Aside from the fact that they make great companions, they are also great lawn mowers and produce a good amount of manure.

There are a few concerns with miniature livestock making their way into the urban set up. One of them is space. You need to have ample space for the livestock to graze. Fenced areas with adequate housing is very important. You also need to have good back up when you need to travel. It is, after all, not as simple as getting your neighbor or friend to take care of your pet dog or cat.

We will deal with these concerns in the following chapters. The thing with miniature pigs is that they are cheaper than their normal sized counterparts but do require good funding in order to raise healthy pets. Only when you are prepared to take good care of them and have the resources to do so should you buy miniature livestock for your home.

Once you have a miniature pig or piglet, they can perform small tasks like drawing carts, which mows your lawn. Of course, they make very loving and gentle pets.

9. Things to know before you buy the micro pig

It is better that you plan the costs that you will incur while raising the micro pig well in advance. This planning will help you to avoid any kind of disappointment that you might face when there are some payments that need to be made. It is better if you plan these costs well in advance, so that you don't get in a fix at the later stage.

There are basically two kinds of costs that you will be looking to incur, which are as follows:

The one-time or initial costs: The initial costs are the costs that you will have to bear in the very beginning of the process of domestication of the animal. This will include the one-time payment that you will give to buy the animal.

There are other costs that would come under this category. The initial costs that you will face when you have decided to domesticate a micro pig are the purchasing cost of the animal, the permits and the license cost, the vaccines, costs of food containers and the costs of the enclosure.

The regular or monthly costs: Even when you are done with the one-time payments, there are some other costs that you won't be able to avoid.

However, these costs can be planned well in advance. You can keep a journal to keep track of these costs.

The monthly costs are the costs that you will have to spend each month or once every few months to raise the micro pig. The costs will include the costs of the food requirements and health requirements of the pet.

The various regular veterinarian visits, the sudden veterinarian visits and replacement of things come under the monthly costs category.

The various costs you can expect

While you are all excited to domesticate the micro pig, you should also start planning for the costs that you will incur. You can expect to incur the following the costs:

Cost of buying the micro pig

If you are planning on buying a micro pig from a pet shop, then you can expect to pay somewhere around $750/£536 to 3000/£2144. However, this is only the buying cost of the micro pig; you will have to pay for the vaccinations of the animal as well. These vaccinations could cost you around $750/£286.

You should make sure that you get the micro pig medically tested before buying it. The examination and tests will also add on to the initial cost. You also have the option of adopting a micro pig. This will help you to avoid the initial buying cost, though the other costs for raising the micro pig will remain essentially the same.

Cost of shelter

When you bring a pet home, you have to make the necessary arrangements to give it a comfortable home. The shelter of the animal will be his home, so it is important that you construct the shelter according to the animal's needs.

This is a one-time cost, so you should not try to save money at the cost of the pet's comfort. The cost of shelter will depend on the type of the shelter. You can expect to spend anywhere between $300/£215 to $400/£286 for the cage of the micro pig.

Cost of food

This is important because if the animal does not get all the appropriate nutrients in the right amount, his health will suffer, which again will be an extra cost for you. So, make sure that you provide all the necessary nutrients to your pet animal.

You should be prepared to spend about $300/£215 on the diet of your pet every month. The costs will vary depending on various factors, such as the brand of products that you choose and also your exact location.

Cost of health care

It is important to invest in the health of a pet animal. This is necessary because an unhealthy animal is the breeding ground of many other diseases in the home. Your pet might pass on the diseases to other pets if not treated on time. This means danger for the pets and also the members of the family.

You will have to take the micro pig to the veterinarian for regular visits. He will be able to guide you regarding any medications and vaccines that the pet may need.

It is advised that for the very first year of domestication, you are extra careful regarding the health of the animal. You should be prepared to spend $300/£215 to $400/£286.

Other costs

Although the main costs that you will encounter while raising your pet have already been discussed, but there will be some extra costs that you will have to take care of. Most of these costs are one-time costs.

You will have to spend money to buy stuff such as micro pig bedding, accessories, food and water bowls and toys for the pet.

You can expect to spend some $300/£215 on these costs. The cost will depend on the wear and tear and the quality of the products. In order to keep track of the costs that could be awaiting you, you should regularly check the various items in the cage of the pet.

10. Bringing home a healthy micro pig

The following pointers will help you to make sure that your future pet is in the prime of its health:

- Even if the animal has had health issues in the past, it can be a matter of concern for you.

- If you are buying an older micro pig, you need to be all the more vigilant because they could carry some infections.

- All good breeders will maintain a health card, which will have all the details of past diseases and infections. This health card will also help you to understand the vaccines cycle of the animal.

- It is important that you closely examine your prospective pet. You should look for any abrasions on his skin.

- His skin should not be torn or bruised anywhere.

- Never accept previous blood tests or the ones provided to you by the breeder. You must invest in a complete test yourself before the mini is delivered.

- You must not accept a delivery at short notice. You must have everything in place on your property for your new pet.

- Do not buy any livestock that is being sold in a hurry.

- Don't rush into a purchase. Plan well and investigate the breeding facility well.

- You should make it a point to check the body temperature of the micro pig. The body temperature should be normal.

- You should closely look for any kind of injuries. If you find anything that does not seem normal, then you need to discuss it with the breeder.

- The micro pig should not have any broken limbs. You should be able to check this manually.

    You should discuss at length about the concerns that you have regarding the micro pig.

- You should follow all the instructions that the doctor gives you because they will be for the benefit of the animal.

- You should only keep the micro pig if you are convinced that you will be able to care for the little animal.

Chapter 2: Owning a micro pig

If you wish to own a micro pig or even if you already own one, it is important to understand the basic characteristics of the animal. You should know what you can expect from the animal and what you can't.

This will help you to tweak the way you behave with the micro pig in the household, which in turn will help to build a strong bond between the micro pig and you.

Micro pigs are known to be very loyal kinds of animals. If they establish a trust factor with you and will always remain loyal to you. This is a great quality to have in a domesticated animal.

Along with being loyal, they are also known to possess great intelligence, which will surprise you.

When the micro pig is in a happy mood, he will jump around the entire space. His unique ways and antics will leave you and the entire family in splits. If you have had a bad day, your pet will surely help you to release all the tension and enjoy life.

They are also very entertaining and playful. You can expect the entire household to be entertained by the unique gimmicks and pranks of the micro pig. If you are looking for a pet that is affectionate, lovable and fun, then the micro pig is the ideal choice for you, as they won't disappoint you.

In spite of all the qualities of the micro pig, it is often termed as a high maintenance pet. If you are still contemplating whether you wish to buy a micro pig or not, then it is important that you understand all about the maintenance of the pet, so that you can make the right choice for yourself.

There are a few considerations that you need to make before you bring a miniature pig home:

- You need to have a large enough space for each member of your herd.

- You must have enough finances to provide good quality food and healthcare for your pets.

- They need to have a place to take shelter and rest.

- You need to be aware of the right way to interact with your miniature pigs to stay safe and to make sure that they animals are not stressed.

There are a few things that you have to keep prepared before you bring your miniature pig home.

1. Where to buy a miniature pig

The first step is to figure out the best source for your miniature pig. The most common options include:

- A breeder: There are commercial and hobby breeders who work towards producing a single breed of mini livestock or try to experiment with different breeds and genetic lines. You need to make sure that the breeder that you are planning to buy from has positive testimonies, maintains a clean and hygienic environment for his pigs and piglets and has ample knowledge about minis.

- A primary owner: Sometimes, owners may be interested in selling or giving away piglets that were born in their yard or farm. These individuals are not breeders and are probably the best source, as they do not have any agenda with their piglets. These people are genuinely concerned about the health and safety of the herd.

- Auctions: In the case of rare breeds, there may be auctions at state shows and fairs. This is risky, as you do not know what health or behavioral issues the pig or piglet may have. Buying from an auction is generally not recommended for first time buyers.

- Rescue/shelter: This is the most economical option available to you. However, the breed may be poor in quality and may come with several health issues as well.

Buying options with mini pigs

When you buy your miniature pig, make sure that you choose the breed according to the purpose that it will serve on your farm. We have discussed the qualities of different breeds in the previous chapter. Since they are extremely expensive, learning all you can about your preferred breed will help you choose a healthy specimen.

Always make sure that you buy from a reputable breeder. Secondly, you must insist on a health check up by a vet before you bring one home.

If you want to get started with your miniature herd right away, you can choose purebred adults and breeding stock. They are the most expensive option and are also not easily available in most cases. You can consider buying piglets because they are more readily available.

The disadvantage with piglets is that they do not come with a breeding guarantee. So if the piglet grows up to be poor in production, you will lose out on your investment. A piglet is a good option if you are not particularly interested in breeding and are looking for a low price option.

For some breeds, it is also possible to purchase the embryos, but you can do so only if you have the knowledge and facilities or necessary assistance for successful embryo transfers in your livestock.

You have the option of buying frozen embryos or one that has been implanted in a female already. The latter is the cheaper and safer option. In the case of embryo implantation, the success rate varies. It is usually about 60% on average.

In case you decide to purchase frozen embryos, you must consider meeting a reproductive specialist who deals with livestock solely. Make sure you gain as much knowledge as possible. It is also important to choose a healthy pig for implantation.

There are many risks with purchasing embryos. The success rate is not 100% to begin with. You also cannot determine the gender of the piglet that will be born. Only when you are looking for an extremely rare breed, you may not have too many other options to pursue.

Adopting a miniature pig

Some farms will put their piglets up for adoption. You may also adopt one from a rescue shelter. With the latter option, be prepared for possible behavioral issues in the pig, as they may have had a history of abuse or poor treatment.

Now, with adoption, you only have to pay an adoption fee for your pig or piglet. This starts as low as $30 or £12 depending upon the medical history of the animal and the expenses borne for the animal.

The pigs or piglets up for adoption will be listed on the website of the shelter or farm that you plan to adopt from. You can look for one with all the desirable traits. Make sure that you visit the animal that you have chosen at least once to ensure that the temperament suits your home. You need to be particularly careful when you are adopting a piglet, as you need to be cautious when you are approaching them, especially during breeding season.

Once you have transferred the adoption fee, you will have to send in all your personal details. They may require a few documents of identity as well. Then, the miniature livestock that you have selected will either be delivered to your home or you may have to pick him up, depending upon the conditions of the place you are adopting from.

Some of them insist on house checks as well. Once the adoption process is complete, it is good to get your pet checked by a vet immediately. In some cases, you will be able to get a health guarantee that allows you to return the animal you adopted, provided he has been checked in less than 72 hours of delivery.

Choosing the best breed

Once you have found a good breeder you can buy a good miniature livestock breed from, the next step is to decide which one suits you best. Each breed has a different requirement and temperament that you need to cater to.

The origin of the breed is the first thing that you must consider. The next thing is to understand the breeds that your mini is a mixture of. This will help broadly determine the characteristics of the breed and the type of environment that you will need to provide.

Your interest in bringing home a miniature pig is also important. The resources available and the type of care that you will be able to provide will also determine which breed you must choose as a pet.

If you are looking for a herd, you need to consider factors like the local climate, the weather pattern, the type of pasture that you have and the space available. Some breeds are adaptable to cold climates, specifically the double coated ones, and others will do well in hot climate.

Try to learn as much as you can about the breed that you have set your mind on. The more you learn, the more you will be able to look into the details of their behavior. For example, Angus livestock are known for their marbling ability while Herefords are known for being placid in nature and also for their high feed efficiency.

If it costs more to feed them, you may not have too much profit. It is best that you find a hardier breed that will be able to function even with marginal pastures if you are looking at a commercial venture. If they are good at calving, you will also see that the pig will stay longer with the herd, providing more milk.

In the end, the only thing that determines what breed that you choose is the purpose of bringing one home. Some are specifically chosen as companions, some make great show animals and some are commercially more viable.

It is recommended that you choose local breeds, as they are likely to adapt faster. They will be able to handle the weather fluctuations and will be healthier. However, with the right resources, you can raise a healthy herd of any breed.

As long as you are willing to learn more and provide for your pet, you can choose any breed for your home. However, do not make a choice because you have a favorite when you also know that it will be a challenge to provide for him or her.

2. Advantages and disadvantages of domesticating micro pigs

If you have already bought or adopted a micro pig, even then this section will help you. The list of pros and cons of micro pigs will help you to prepare yourself for the challenges that lie ahead of you. This list will help you to be a better parent to the pet and to form an ever-lasting bond with your beloved pet.

Advantages of domesticating a micro pig:

If you are still not sure about adopting or buying a micro pig, then you should know that there are many pros of domesticating a micro pig. They are loved by their owners and their families because of some amazing qualities that they possess.

This animal can definitely prove to be a great pet for your household and your family.

The various advantages of domesticating a micro pig are as follows:

- The size of the micro pig makes it an ideal choice as a pet.

- Their looks make them adorable and cute to look at. They are loved by all. Who wouldn't want to have a pet that is beautiful to look at?

- People who love pets that can be lifted and cuddled will love the micro pig. A micro pig will allow you to lift it and play with it.

- This pet will be the center of affection for all the family members and also for each and every visitor of the house.

- Micro pigs are known to be very loyal animals. They will want your presence around them and will show you that they love you in their own unique ways.

- If they establish a trust factor with you, they will always remain loyal to you. Loyalty is a very good trait in an animal. This is a great quality to have in a domesticated animal.

- Micro pigs are also known to possess great intelligence. You should be prepared to witness their intelligent antics and gimmicks. They will actually surprise you with their intelligence and smartness.

- A micro pig is a very sharp animal. It is always good to have a pet that is intelligent and sharp.

- If you care well for the pet, he will also respond in a very positive way. When the micro pig is in a happy mood, he will jump around the entire space. His unique ways and antics will leave you in splits.

- They are very entertaining. They have a habit of themselves and also people around them. If you just sit around a micro pig, you are bound to have a great time.

- If there are kids in your home, they will fall in love with this pet. However, you should monitor the interaction of the kids with the pet. This is important to keep everyone safe and sound.

- Micro pigs don't overeat, so you don't have to worry about this aspect. You can leave food in the container and the micro pig will eat as much is required. They are used to eating several small meals.

- The micro pigs can be trained. You can teach them some easy tricks to have more fun with them.

- A very important point to note here is that their demeanor will depend a lot on how they are raised. The preparation has to begin right from the start. You can't expect them to suddenly become friendly after years of wrong treatment. If they are raised to be social, they will be very social.

- Micro pigs live in groups in their natural environment. This makes them tolerant towards other micro pigs. The micro pigs will wrestle and play with each other. There is a very slight possibility that they will not get along.

- Micro pigs have a fairly long life, if they are taken care of. You can make a strong emotional bond with your pet and can enjoy the fruits of the bond for years to come.

Disadvantages of domesticating a micro pig:

The adorable and friendly animal has his own set of challenges when it comes to domesticating. It is important to understand these disadvantages so that you can be better prepared for them. Following are the disadvantages of raising a micro pig:

- Miniature livestock can be pricey. In order to get started, you will have to make a big investment.

- Micro pigs are considered very high maintenance. You should be ready to spend money and time on these pets.

- The eyesight of pigs is very poor. They are almost blind. This can be a real challenge for most owners. They indulge in rooting habits to locate food. This can be very messy.

- Though the animal is miniature, you can expect it to attain a weight of over 50 pounds. This can be a problem for many. If you are looking for an animal that is less in weight, then you will be disappointed.

- They are definitely not suitable for someone who is looking for a quiet and calm pet. They are energetic, will run around and will also make noises.

- Because of his energy levels, the micro pig can run into things and can get hurt very easily.

- The animal seeks a lot of attention. Micro pig is a kind of pet that will require you to pamper him a lot.

- The pet can get stressed and depressed if he is left alone for longer durations. You can't leave him in the cage for too long.

- The cost that you will incur while buying and raising is more when compared to other pets, such as the dog and the cat.

- The pet has a very inactive lifestyle. This can lead to many health issues.

- The pet is prone to stress. This can also lead to many diseases and health related issues in the pet animal.

4. Transport and handling

Once you have decided the breed of miniature livestock that you want to bring home, you can look for a reliable source. The next thing that you should do is to make sure that you transport your livestock in the right way to reduce any stress that is related to travelling.

There are legal considerations when you transport livestock to make it a more humane process. According to the Code of Accepted Farm Practice for the Welfare of Livestock, here are a few things that you need to keep in mind when you are brining your pet home:

The transport vehicle should be of the appropriate size and design to make sure that your entire stock can be transported comfortably.

The transport vehicle should be in good condition. That way, you will not have any injuries due to protrusions or other issues in the container. You can also ensure that the livestock will reach the destination on time without any delay due to breakdowns.

The stock crate should be examined thoroughly. It should be smooth and the contact surface should not have any protrusions.

In case the transport crate has any pens, they should not be more than 3 meters in length. That way the animals will have enough support during the travel and will also feel less stressed as a result of that.

It is best that you hire a trailer or a transport truck for your mini livestock. The front of the trailer should be solid enough to protect the piglet from any wind. The animal that is being transported should be checked on at least every 3 hours.

You must feed the animal 6 hours before you transport him or her. The number of animals in the trailer should be such that they can lie down when they are being transported.

Never transport a mini pig or piglet in the boot of your car or in a sealed container that does not allow air flow. The legs of the animals must never be tied to restrain them.

The trailer should never be overloaded. Even if it means that you may have to make multiple trips, the trailer should only have as many as it can accommodate comfortably.

These simple precautions will ensure that your miniature pig does not feel very stressed after the journey. That way, it will be easy for you to introduce the animal into your property on the first day.

5. Introducing your new livestock to an existing herd

If you already have a small herd or miniature livestock or regular sized livestock, proper introduction is the key to maintaining peace within the herd. What you can be sure of is that there will not be any ugly fights.

They tend to establish the pecking order quite peacefully. Yet, with introduction of new livestock, the biggest concern is potential health risks to the existing herd.

You need to make sure that all precautions are taken before you allow your new pet to graze with the existing herd or even stay with them in the same housing area.

Precautions to avoid diseases

Even when you have the healthiest miniature pig added to the property, you must remember that the immunity of the animal will be compromised because of the transport stress, the new environment and the change in food and water. This is one of the main reasons why you need to take all the precautions possible before you introduce the animal to the existing herd.

Even before you transport the new pig, you need to have a complete blood test done. Look for an authorized lab or consult your vet before you agree to buy a mini.

It is advisable to keep your new pig quarantined in a separate enclosure for a minimum of 14 days. It is better if you can quarantine for 60 days. This will give the new animal ample time to get accustomed to the new place and will also give you a chance to observe closely for any signs of disease.

Introduction to the herd

For the most part, your mini will be safe in a herd when introduced. Livestock seldom get into aggressive fights, but if you have regular sized pigs and piglets in your herd, taking precautions is necessary. The sheer size of the other animals can lead to dominant behavior.

A temporary fence can be placed between the new pet and the existing herd when you let them all out to graze. Supervise the herd during this period to see how they respond. If they are not very alert and practically ignore the newcomer, it is a good sign. You can keep them in adjacent pastures for a few days to help them get used to the smell and sight of one another. This is recommended especially if you are introducing a piglet to a herd that already has a mature piglet.

It is a good idea to avoid any introduction of a new piglet during the mating season. This can lead to some squabbles. When you let the new member interact with the herd without a fence, it should be monitored at all times initially. If there is any sign of head butting or chasing, you must isolate the new pig or piglet immediately.

When you feel like the herd is getting along with the new member, allow short unsupervised introductions. Leave them together for half an hour and come back to check on them. This time period can increase slowly as they get used to each other.

It is advisable to separate polled and horned animals. If possible, you can have a separate herd of miniature pigs and one with regular sized pigs. That way, there is no room for dominant behavior at any point.

If you do notice any bruises or cuts, contact your vet to understand the source. This also brings us to an important point of introducing the new member to the herd on a weekday. That way, you can be sure that the vet is available in case there is any untoward incident or injury to the new animal.

6. Introducing a mini to other animals

If you have a pet dog at home, it is necessary to make the introduction correctly. With pets like cats, the risk is lower, as they will not approach the pig or piglet in most cases. The interactions are also limited because of the nature of cats. That said, even cats must not be left unsupervised with your pigs. The size difference means that the cat is at the risk of being kicked or trampled if he startles the pig.

With dogs, they usually run around in the yard and will frequently interact with your new miniature pig, so proper introductions are necessary.

The first introduction should be with your dog on a leash. Watch the dog's reaction. Frothing at the mouth, the tail pointing upwards or a hunting position means that your dog is in an attack mode. This is natural the first time they meet. If you can calm your dog down and let him watch the pigs while on a leash, do so. If not, try to introduce them again.

With frequent meetings, the dogs will become less responsive in an aggressive manner. It is still not safe to let the dog run freely around the pig. To begin with, the dog has a natural predatory instinct towards a pig. Second, a startled pig can cause serious damage to a dog with one single blow with his strong legs.

Allow them to interact with a temporary fence between them. Keep an eye on your dog's reaction. With regular and controlled meetings, the dog will begin to ignore the pig and lose interest in it completely.

Only a dog who is obedience trained is safe to leave with the pigs without any barrier. The most important commands that your dog must respond to are stay and come. If you do not get your dog to respond every time, work on his obedience skills before he is let out with the pigs.

Some livestock owners and farm owners suggest an e-collar to prevent any attacks. However, the safer way and the gentler option is to train your dog to obey commands flawlessly. This is one of the most important things for dogs that will work on farms. Once they are trained and comfortable, you can even get your dog to herd livestock for you and keep them from escaping from your farm or yard.

Special training is available for herding dogs. You can look for trainers who will help you with this and make your dog an important part of your journey with your miniature pig.

If you are lucky, the first interaction itself will be calm and easy. If not, work with your dog and help him make new friends.

Chapter 3: Decoding the micro pig's behavior

A micro pig is a small, naughty animal that will keep you busy and entertained by all its unique antics and mischiefs. It is said that each animal is different from the other. Each one will have some traits that are unique to him.

While you will learn about all the unique traits that your particular micro pig has by experiencing him and spending time with him, there are some traits that almost all micro pigs will exhibit. It is beneficial to know of these traits so that you are not taken off guard. You will be able to understand what is normal for this animal and what is not.

There is no doubt that miniature pigs make great pets. They are affectionate and are also extremely friendly. You can find a great companion in your miniature pig provided you spend some time to understand their behavior and make a connection.

Miniature pigs are known to be great show animals. This means that they can also be trained with ease with some commitment. This section explains the general behavior of pigs and piglets to help you understand how have more positive interactions with your pet and also stay safe when doing so.

1. Understanding behavior of your miniature pig

In the case of miniature livestock, you need to be aware of all the senses that they use. There is more to livestock than just vision. This is the key to proper interaction without startling the animal.

The different senses

The eyes of livestock are placed on the side of the head. This gives them a combination of binocular and panoramic vision. With this, they are able to stay aware of any predator. There is a blind spot just behind them. The eye muscles of livestock are generally weaker, which means that they cannot focus on any object immediately.

They can distinguish between a few colors like red, orange and yellow better than the short wavelength colors like blue and green. This helps them survive in the wild, as they are able to see blood in an instant if any herd member has been attacked by a predator. They do not have great depth perception. This is the reason for one of the most common issues with mini livestock, which is refusing to step over a drain gate or to cross an area with a shadow.

Sniffing the pasture is common for pigs when they are grazing but it is not certain if smell is a really important sense. They have been seen to baulk at the smell of offal or blood. They also have a secondary olfactory or sense of smell that helps them identify pheromones

The ears are the most sensitive of all sense organs. It is possible to calm your mini with some soothing music. At the same time, any loud noise can cause a lot of stress, so approaching a pig when talking loudly or yelling in an excited tone can make your pig react in a negative manner.

Livestock have something called a flight zone. This is the "comfort zone" of your pig. If the pig has been fed in a feed lot this is about 1.5 m around them and in the case of livestock that is not handled too frequently, it is about 30m.

When anyone unfamiliar enters this flight zone, the livestock will either move away or just let you know that you are not welcome. This is why you need to work towards the right methods of approaching your mini. Although they are extremely gentle, getting them worked up is never a good plan.

2. Reading pig or piglet's behavior

Even in some of the most well established farms, people are seldom aware of the right way to approach livestock. This results in animals that are extremely stressed and uncomfortable. It affects their productivity and in worst cases can provoke an attack from the animal.

Reading the body language of your pet can really help you create that special bond that you dream of. For instance, if a pig is relaxed, he will stretch after standing up. If he is under any kind of stress, the common behavior includes bellowing, butting and even kicking. These behaviors are clear indicators that the immediate environment needs to be changed.

The tail is one of the best indicators of the mental state of the animal. If it hangs straight down, the pig is very relaxed and is just going about its routine. If the tail is tucked in between the legs, it is an indication of fear, illness or cold weather. If the tail hangs away from the body, it is a sign of caution or threat. You know that your pig is in a playful mood if he is running with the tail held out. There is a slight kink as opposed to the absolutely straight tail.

3. Threat behavior

If you have a pig, you will have to deal less with any threat per say. The body language is almost similar to that of a piglet. But, what is important to understand is that piglets are more likely to display behavior that warns you of an attack. If you are dealing with a piglet in heat, especially, you must watch out for these signs.

Piglets have some common behaviors such as challenging, threatening, female seeking, nudging and territorial behavior. No matter what the cause is, a piglet will provide a threat display because he is in a state of fight or flight.

When he shows a threat display, he will arch the broad side of his back to look bigger. Then, the head will be lowered and may be accompanied by rapid side to side movement. The hair on the back will stand and the eyeballs protrude when the piglet is threatening you.

You must read a direct threat when the shoulders are hunched with the neck curved and the head lowered. The neck tilts towards the object that is being threatened. Then, the piglet will paw his forefeet to send some mud or dirt flying back. He will also horn the ground or rub it.

If you move away when this display is on, you will probably have no further interaction. On the other hand, if you keep approaching the piglet, he will end up fighting with the horns and his head.

When you see this display, it is best that you exit as fast as possible. You need to get at least 20m away from the piglet if you want him to ignore you fully.

With piglets, behavior may change per the season. For example, when a pig in heat is nearby, he will be more defensive. So, you must never expect a certain behavior even if the piglet has been extremely gentle with you. Watch for signs and move away when you have to. It is best that you keep a piglet with a mate or in a herd. Interacting with a lone piglet is often considered harmful. You must also never turn your back to the piglet. If you are milking a pig, the piglets must be restrained away from her.

The better your interactions get, the calmer your animal will be. Never tease a piglet for instance. Rubbing the horn area or the head or petting the pig like you would pet a dog is never a good idea.

If you want to pet your pig or piglet, stroking behind the ears or under the chin can be very comforting.

4. Approaching a pig or piglet correctly

A method known as low stress livestock handling is the best approach to handling livestock. You need to study the animal first and then prepare the animal for your approach. There are many reasons why you will have to approach the pig or piglet besides petting and playing.

You have to let them out into the pasture for grazing, feed them, move them when you have to clean the housing area and lead them into a vehicle in case they need to be transported for a vet visit or any other purpose. In no scenario do you want to startle the animal and cause unruly behavior. Even a miniature pig is a lot to handle when he is in a flight mode.

Most owners make a mistake in the approach. This can sometimes lead to bad behavior all day long or may lead to an immediate negative reaction.

When you see a cute mini Hereford or Dexter, it is natural for you to make sounds that are excited. Normally people move head on and try to touch the animal. Remember the flight zone. When you continue to approach it, the animal feels threatened.

This makes the animal perceive you as a threat. Naturally, they will get upset, uneasy or angry. These are emotions that they cannot handle. Pigs are prey animals and anyone who approaches them displays the same behavior as a predator. A predator will just move head on and attempt to catch prey.

Even circling your pig is a predator behavior that makes them react to you negatively.

Now, imaging that you are driving on a freeway and a car is moving towards you in a straight line. The first reaction that you will have is that of fear. Now, if the car changes the line of movement and you notice that it is turning or moving around you, you become calm. The fear reaction can be intense or mild depending upon the speed of the approaching vehicle.

We calculate the angle that the car is approaching us at and decide if it will be a hit or a miss. This is exactly how your pig will react if you walk straight towards them. It is a good idea to get close enough to the animal so that we do not enter that pressure zone and then move in an oblique direction.

This straight to oblique path will let the animal remain calm and comfortable. This is the same principle that you will apply even to a pig that you know well and even older pigs who are extremely docile generally.

The next question is, how do you know when you are in the flight zone? It is quite simple. When you get to this zone is when the animal will take notice of you for the first time. You will see them looking at you or trying to move away. This is when you will change your angle or just stop in place. The goal is to make sure that they do not move away from you. The moment you see an alert body language is when you make the change in your path.

When you do this regularly, they learn that when they feel the pressure of you approaching them, this will be released by you on your own. They will learn that they do not have to move away in order to be safe. They know now that you will not get so close that it will bother them. When you fail to do this, the animal will feel the need to run. If there are piglets in the herd, the female will feel a lot more pressure as she cannot leave her little one behind.

Read the signs exhibited by the animal and adjust your movement. When you pig becomes familiar with your presence, you can get closer each time until you can get close enough to touch her without really scaring her.

Never move towards the animal with your hand held out. This looks like you are about to attack. The other thing that you need to keep in mind is that you must never hold any object that will make you look larger. This includes sticks, a baseball bat or any other object that adds height. The bigger the approaching object, the more nervous the pig is going to get.

You will also avoid any sudden movements like waving the hand, opening your arms out to hug the animal or running. The calmer you are, the calmer your pet will be. If you have visitors or children who want to meet the pig, you have to be strict about the way they approach her. If they leave the animal in a bad mood, you will have to deal with her all day long. Worse still, if the animal gets into a flight mode, they may head butt or kick in defense. You must be extra cautious when you approach a piglet.

Chapter 4: Setting up the micro pig's home

Like you need a home, an animal also needs a place and space that he can call his home. A home should make him happy and should be inviting for him. When the home does not provide the comfort and security that it should, it can lead to detrimental results.

There are many owners who might feel that there is no need to set up a cage because the pet can stay indoors. However, you need to remember that even if you are a hands-on parent of the pet, there will be times when the pet would be unsupervised.

There will be times when you will have to concentrate on some other work and the micro pig would be alone. The cage is very handy at such times because you can do your work and can also be sure that you pet is safe and sound in the cage that you have built for him.

In addition, during the night time, it is best for the pet and also for the family members that the pet sleeps in his cage. The pet will get used to the cage and your family members can also sleep without any tensions of your pet being loose in the house.

When you are setting up a cage for the micro pig, you need to make sure that the cage is set up in a way that is inviting for the micro pig. The micro pig should not feel like a captive or a prisoner in the cage. If the micro pig is not comfortable, he will begin to get stressed, which is something that you wouldn't want.

The cage should be built keeping in mind the basic nature of the micro pig. You can't build a cage that is suitable for a tiger or a bird. You have a micro pig and your cage should be built keeping in mind his natural behavior, instincts, likes and dislikes. This is the best for you and also for the micro pig.

You should understand that just because the micro pig is a small animal does not mean that you can keep it anywhere. You need a proper cage for him. You should never keep him in a glass environment such as an aquarium. Such places don't allow the flow of air and can cause breathing issues in the micro pig.

It is important to have the right temperature for the micro pig. If the temperature is more than eighty degrees Fahrenheit or less than forty five degrees Fahrenheit, it is advised to keep the pet inside the house in controlled temperatures. Nothing is more important than the health and well-being of the pet.

There are different ways of keeping a herd. You can either have an extensive area for grazing or can keep the herd in close confinement. But, it is your responsibility to make sure that you provide for the welfare of your herd. The basic needs such as food, fresh air, clean water and shelter. In fact not providing ample shelter from extreme weather conditions will lead to animal cruelty in many states.

A healthy herd can tolerate weather changes to a large extent provided they have good access to fresh water and food and have been acclimatized. In any case, providing shelter will ensure that no production ability is lost. When the herd does not have enough shelter, a lot of their energy goes into just taking care of normal functions.

If the temperature goes above or below the average temperature that the animal can handle, you have to make sure that you provide them with adequate shelter. It is possible for deaths to occur in your herd because of extreme weather conditions.

1. Dealing with adverse weather

Any extremities including temperature dropping suddenly or increasing suddenly can be categorized as adverse weather. This includes wind and rain, sudden drop in temperatures or heat waves. Miniature livestock have ways of dealing with this naturally but when the temperatures are too extreme, they need adequate shelter.

Coping with heat

Respiration is the primary method of heat loss in livestock. They also transfer the heat into the air and cool off when sweat evaporates. You need to provide shelter that will protect the animals from direct sunlight. That way the heat load reduces by almost 50%. This ensures that your livestock does not have any exhaustion due to heat stress.

Pregnant livestock and piglets are at the highest risk of dying due to a heat shock. This is because they have lower heat resistance. This is also true with any livestock that may have respiratory diseases.

When shade is available, you will see that livestock will rest during the warmer parts of the day and will only graze as the day gets cooler.

If your farm or yard does not have any trees, they will spend time near any water source and will only feed at night. Research shows that shade is preferred over water because that allows the livestock to spend more time resting.

The animals that are at risk of heat-related stress are:

- Young animals

- Animals with darker color

- Animals with poor health

- Obese stock.

The best shelter options in hot weather conditions

If you live in a part of the world that tends to have warmer weather, you can choose the following options:

- Shade belts: This includes a line of deciduous trees that are planted in the east-west direction. That provides shade on the southern part. You can prune the trees regularly to help improve air circulation.

- Constructed shelters that usually include wooden or iron poles with a roof of shade cloth, timber or iron.

- You can even plant trees that have large canopies. These trees will give the area a cooling effect thanks to the absorption of heat by the leaves.

Make sure that your livestock has enough water to drink during the warmer months. As a rule, miniature livestock will consume close to 100 liters of water. This will increase when the temperature increases to above 335 degrees C.

Keep the water source close to the shelter so that the livestock can get familiar with it. The volume of the water container should be high enough to cope with demanding conditions. If you have a mixed barn, you have to increase the number of watering points and also improve the water quantity as the temperature increases.

Coping with cold weather

Just like hot weather, cold weather also causes a lot of stress. Cold weather accompanied by rain will reduce the body temperature of the animal. Livestock that are at high risk of cold related stress are:

- New born piglets or pregnant pigs

- Sick animals

- Animals that have a low body condition.

In these animals, cold can also lead to death if it is too extreme. During cold weather, there is an increase in appetite as the animals will need more energy in order to maintain normal body temperature.

This means that the food that you provide should be highly digestible. It also helps to increase the quantity of food that your miniature livestock finds more palatable. Of course, good shelter helps reduce cold stress **effectively.**

2. The best shelter options in cold weather conditions

The shelter that you provide must be able to protect the animals from the cold. Some of the best options are:

- Shelters with wind breaks. You will see that the livestock will rub up against the wind break to stay strong, so you need to make sure that the wind break should be strong and safe.

- If you have a shelterbelt of trees, it will be able to keep the livestock safe from winds. There is a shelter zone that is usually up to about 14 times the height of the shelterbelt.

- Make sure that there are trees in the north-south direction as most wind flow will be in the north and south western direction.

- Paddocks and gullies make good shelter against cold.

When you plant a shelter belt, make sure that the trees are spaced out evenly. That ensures wind flow without too much turbulence.

You must not allow any pregnant livestock to graze in paddocks that have Yellow or Monterey pine trees. If the fallen branches and twigs are ingested, it poses great threat to the fetus.

You can build one-sided sheds for your livestock. Temporary shelter can be built using plastic tarpaulins and shade cloth if you do not have any other shelter option.

Shelter is one of the most important parts of proper husbandry of miniature livestock

3. Building housing areas

Shelterbelts cannot be created overnight. It may take several months for the shelterbelt to grow properly. If you do not have trees to protect your miniature livestock during adverse weather conditions, here are a few housing options that you can try:

- **Single slope, open sided sheds:** This is the most typical housing option. It is suitable for any livestock that you have on your farm. It is easy to build and is also economical. When you build an open sided shelter, make sure that the open end faces south in the winter to block any wind. You also have the option of partitioning the pole barns to make sure that the animals are kept at a distance easily.

- **Clear span open sided shelter:** When you have a clear span, you have ample space to use manure removal equipment. You can open any side of this shelter as per the weather. You have a gable end that should be open when there is any rain or snow. With the gable end open, you have more depth in the bay area, protecting the animal from winds. The back end of this shelter may become damp and will require ventilation and lighting. This is perfect if you have a herd that is smaller than 20 in number.

- **An unused barn:** This structure can be built but it is a better option if you already have one on your farm. You can renovate it as per the requirement of your miniature livestock. This is cheaper than installing a whole new structure. That is why it is recommended that you have a free stall barn instead of a conventional tie stall.

- **Hoop barn:** This is possibly the most expensive type of shelter for your livestock, but it does provide a lot of protection in cold conditions. However, in the warmer months, ventilation can be a problem. If you have ample grazing space for your livestock, this is not really a big concern. A hoop barn looks almost like a greenhouse with a roof that is arched.

When you are constructing a shelter or housing area for your livestock, here are a few things that you must consider:

- Make sure that the design is simple and practical to maintain it well.

- You must have enough space to make a feed yard to keep the animals comfortable and socialize properly.

- The flooring should be covered with some substrate that can absorb waste. The best option is hay. Mud is not a good idea, especially in winter. Evaporation is lower with mud and if the draining is improper, it can harbor several microbes. If the floor is already made of mud, adding bedding like hay can be a good option.

- The selected area for housing should be higher than the rest of the land. That will help you get rainwater and waste out easily.

- There should be ample light and air supply in the shelter. Sunlight is extremely necessary to keep the shelter dry and prevent any germs or viruses from breeding.

- Try to build a shelter in an area that is surrounded by trees. This helps provide additional shade and shelter to the animals.

- There should be a good drainage system inside the shelter to make sure that there is no dampness whatsoever. Trash and excreta in the shelter will lead to the growth of virus, parasites and insects like mosquitos and flies. They transmit diseases that can affect the entire herd in some cases.

- The shelter should be covered with some form of fencing. We will discuss the options in the next section.

- Make sure that every animal has a least five square meters of space inside the housing area in order to prevent overcrowding and related stress.

- It is a good idea to create a separate area of housing to keep any injured or sick animal. This should be a quiet and dry area to prevent any stress.

You must keep the shelter ready before you bring your miniature pig home. Make sure that it suits the requirements based on the number of livestock and even the age and gender. Younger livestock and piglets will need a shelter that is stronger as they tend to have more energy, which means that they are able to apply more force on the walls.

4. Best fencing options

Proper fencing is necessary in order to keep your livestock from entering any unsafe area on your property or from walking out onto a busy street. It also ensures that your livestock is safe from any predators.

You also need good fencing to manage grazing. You can control the area that your livestock grazes in so that they only get access to good fodder. This can be done with the help of temporary fencing. Permanent fences are usually used to mark the boundaries of your property.

Whether you are choosing temporary or permanent fencing, here are the options available:

- **Barbed wire fence:** This type of fence consists of several strands of horizontal wire that has barbs every 12 cm. Do not use wires that have barbs placed closer, as it can lead to injuries.

- **Woven wire fence:** This type of fence contains smooth steel wires that are woven with horizontal and vertical wires. This is one of the most widely used type of fencing. However, it is expensive and may not be as useful as high tensile wires.

- **High tensile wires:** You can choose either electric or non-electric fencing. It is more elastic, is lighter and more effective.

- **Interior fencing:** This may include a temporary electric fence or may use a permanent fence that divides the area. This helps livestock stay in one area without any conflict or territorial behavior.

It is common practice to use electric wires, but make sure that your livestock is trained to recognize the electric fence before you introduce them into a pasture with this type of fencing. You can start by using one strand of hot wire at very low voltage near the water sources. Even a mild current is enough for the livestock to recognize an electric fence and make sure that they stay clear of it.

5. Cleaning the housing area

A clean housing area is essential for proper hygiene. If you have piglets, pregnant pigs or animals with a low body condition, you need to be extra cautious, as they have very little immunity to infections and illnesses.

The housing area can get dirty really quickly considering that there is going to be a lot of manure and other debris that gets accumulated over time. While you can have a bedding material that is absorbent, it is necessary to change it and clean the housing area regularly.

If there are any organisms in the housing area, there is also a chance that the milk that you consume will get contaminated. Then the shelf life of milk reduces and it may even transmit diseases to the people who consume the milk.

The floor needs to be kept dry at all times to make sure that the animals do not get any foot infection or injury. Insects are also a health hazard. It disturbs the animals to begin with and also spreads diseases in the herd very fast.

How to clean the shed

You need to be willing to use water liberally to thoroughly clean a pig's housing area. You need to have the right equipment such as a wheel barrow in order to lift and dispose of the bedding and the waste after it has been cleaned. The housing area needs good drainage so that you can remove liquid waste properly.

It is a good idea to remove fodder and feed that is remaining in the manger. This will reduce any chance of fly-related nuisances. When you clean the entire area with water periodically, you can eliminate bacteria, algae, any chance of viral contamination or fungi. That way you can prevent most health issues that pigs are prone to.

What sanitizer to use

One of the best and most potent sanitizers is sunlight. It has the ability to destroy all organisms that produce diseases. The goal of disinfecting a shed is to make it free from any microbe that causes diseases. You can sprinkle the area with the following chemical agents for best results:

- **Bleaching powder:** This compound consists of almost 39% calcium. It is one of the best and most easily available chemicals.

- **Iodophor and iodine:** You can look for commercially made iodophor. This contains 2% iodine and is very effective against germs.

- **Sodium carbonate:** If you decide to use this disinfectant, you can use a hot solution containing 4% sodium carbonate. It will wash away certain strains of bacteria and several viruses.

- **Slaked lime and quick lime:** These ingredients are used to whitewash the walls of the housing area. They prevent several microbes from breeding in the first place.

- **Phenol:** Also known as carbolic acid, this is a common household disinfectant that also works against fungus along with several strains of bacteria.

- **Insecticides:** As the name suggests, these chemicals are effective against insects such as ticks and flies that normally transmit diseases. You can use insecticides on the crevices of walls and cracks as well. You can make a solution of these insecticides and use them to spray and disinfect the most common harboring areas for these insects. Using a powerful sprayer works best, although you can use a brush, sponge or a hand sprayer. The commonly used insecticides are gramazane powder, BHC, DDT, surriithion and malathion. Making a 50% concentrate solution is recommended. However, these insecticides can also be poisonous to livestock, so take care that they do not come into contact with milk, water or any food material.

The right cleaning procedures

- First, the excrement should be removed from the urine channel and the floor. You can use an iron basket and a shovel to pick the dung up. Then transfer it on to a wheel barrow. While doing this, also remove any leftovers or bedding material.

- The water trough should be emptied. A floor brush should be used to scrape the bottom and the sides.

- The water trough should then be washed with clean water. It is recommended that you white wash the water trough with the above mentioned lime solution.

- The floor of the housing area must be scrubbed clean using a broom and a brush. Then you can wash it off with water.

- There may be splashes of excrement on the wall, poles, railing and other structures. This should be scrubbed and cleaned fully.

- If there are any cobwebs, remove them with a wall brush. You must remove cobwebs periodically to prevent any allergic reaction.

- Once the housing area has been washed thoroughly, you can use disinfecting agents like phenol, bleaching powder or washing soda to sprinkle the whole surface.

Precautions

To make sure that the cleaning process is safe, here are a few tips that you can use:

- The bedding material and the excrement should be removed completely.

- If any excrement or bedding material spills when you are carrying it out, make sure that you clean it up instantly.

- Dirty water should never be used to clean the shed.

- If there is any fodder left over, clean it before replacing it with fresh fodder. Never put fresh fodder over the left overs.

- Watch for any growth of algae in the water troughs.

- The concentration of the disinfectants should be correct to make sure that they are actually effective. You also need the right concentration to prevent any chances of poisoning or toxicosis in livestock.

Before you add the new bedding material, make sure that the housing area is fully dry. During the rainy season, it is a good idea to spray any insecticide regularly. This will keep flies at bay. You may even consider whitewashing regularly to keep the mites and ticks in the walls at bay.

Cleaning the housing area once every week is recommended. If not, you must at least clear out the bedding material and wash the housing area thoroughly every fifteen days. This will prevent any unpleasant odor in the area. The more frequently you clean, the easier it is each time.

Chapter 5: Breeding and Reproduction in micro pigs

With miniature livestock, there are several breeding programs that are available. There are continuous attempts to create new breeds of miniature livestock, but if you are a novice with miniature pigs, the first thing that you need to learn is to identify sexual behavior, take care of the pregnant pig and then ensure safe calving.

1. Sexual behavior in livestock

On average, miniature livestock live up to 12-18 years of age. They will become sexually mature when they are about 12-14 months old. From then on, your pig will be able to have one piglet every year. In the case of piglets, they are sexually active until the age of 17.

When the pig goes into heat or estrus, the male pig in your herd will also become excited. He will stay close to the pig and will often be seen smelling the genital area of the pig.

This is a natural way of transferring pheromones. You will see other behavior such as resting the chin on the rump of the pig, snorting and pawing the ground. This behavior indicates that the pig is going to copulate with the female in some time. The copulation itself lasts for a few seconds.

If you have a herd, there is a social ranking within it in most cases. The pigs that are most dominant will display maximum mating.

You will be able to identify a pig in heat because she will get very excited. Then, there will be several attempts made by the male pig to mount her. The level of excitement when the pig is in heat can either be strong, weak or medium. The difference lies in the breed of the pig, the age and just the individual personality of the animal.

If there are castrated miniature pigs in your herd, they will display sexual behavior that is similar to the intact ones. However, he will not be able to copulate because the androgens in the body are not present.

In the case of the females, the endocrine balance determines the type of behavior exhibited. Now, there are several ovarian secretions that will determine the behavior, but estrogen plays the most important role with respect to this.

There are many other factors that determine the level of sexual behavior such as the environment, genetics, the health of the animal, physiological factors and the past experiences.

For instance, pigs that belong to certain breeds tend to be sexually more active than those that belong to the pork breed. If you have new herd members, pigs or piglets, they will get more sexual attention.

So if you have any pig that is not displaying proper breeding behavior, you can introduce a new member to the herd. If all the pigs are sexually healthy, introducing a new animal during the breeding season is never recommended.

The sexual receptivity remains for about 19 hours. When the pigs are receptive, they may mount other pigs or they may be mounted by other pigs as well. When the female is being mounted, she gets into a rigid stance and the process is complete in less than a few seconds.

The gestation period of a miniature pig lasts for 285, days which is the same as the regular sized pig. During this period, proper care and nutrition is necessary. If your pig is giving birth for the first time, the term used to describe her is "heifer".

2. Caring for a pregnant pig

A pregnant pig should be kept in a separate enclosure during the third trimester. Nutrition in the pregnant pig is very important to make sure that the piglets develop properly. It is also essential to prevent possible diseases like Bovine Respiratory disease in the piglet that is born.

On most farms, the common practice is to reduce feed costs with low cost feed. You definitely do not want to do that to your pet, especially when she is pregnant. You need to make sure that she gets the necessary amount of protein, carbohydrates, macro and micro nutrients.

According to the National Research Council, low quality hay does not provide the amount of protein that is necessary for a lactating or pregnant pig.

In addition to this, when the protein level is reduced, the pig may even reduce the intake of food because of an inefficiency of digestion, as the rumen microbial populations are unable to perform efficiently.

When the food intake is reduced, the amount of energy that the pig gets is also reduced, leading to poor development of the fetus.

You need to understand how to check for the quality of the food and combine the feed in such a way that the nutritional requirements are fully met. If you figure out that the food that you are providing is not able to provide the required nutrients, you can even consult your vet to figure out strategies to provide supplementation.

Importance of protein

It has been noticed that when a pig is provided with low quality forage, it leads to a lot of nutritional imbalance. In general, it contains less than 7% protein. If your mini belongs to a meat producing breed, the protein requirement is much higher.

In the case of pigs, they cannot provide maximum performance if the protein in their body is inadequate while all the other nutrients are being provided.

If you figure out that the quality of fodder that you are providing is low, then you will have to give the pig a protein supplement in the later part of the pregnancy to ensure that the nutrient requirements are met.

Mineral nutrition

The metabolism of a pig can only be sustained if she is able to get enough micro and macro nutrients. They play a very important role in the formation of bones, are important components in the hormones and result in the secretion of hormones, maintenance of water balance and amino acid components. They also act as anti-oxidants.

Pigs need at least 17 different minerals including Zinc, chromium, selenium, iron, manganese, etc. just before calving.

Although this has not been investigated thoroughly, it is suggested that the immunity of the piglet can be compromised to a large extent if the pregnant pig does not have access to these minerals. This increases the incidence of diseases like Bovine Respiratory Disorder.

The forage that you supply accounts for a part of the mineral requirement of pigs. If there is any deficiency, it can be managed with mineral supplements that are recommended by the vet. The level of trace minerals in the blood can be evaluated to monitor the level of deficiency in the pig before calving.

Although there is no solid evidence to suggest that nutrition and the immune function of the piglet are interrelated, it has been concluded that the improper secretion of antibodies and hormones in the piglet can compromise the immune system.

The colostrum of "first milk" after the piglet is born transfers a lot of immunoglobulins to the piglet. This helps prevent diseases and keeps the piglet protected for at least 24 hours after birth. If the piglet is not given the colostrum, they are at risk of developing several complications that will lead to poor body conditions and expensive treatment procedures as well.

Besides proper nutrition, you will also have to make the environment of the pregnant pig free from any stressors. This includes noises or other animals. You must provide her with a quiet corner. This is especially needed in the last trimester, when the pig can start to get a little uncomfortable.

When your pig is ready to give birth, it is best that you leave her alone and let nature take its course. Sometimes, the pig may need assistance. We will discuss how you can help deliver the piglet. In case you are unsure of this, you can speak to your vet for more assistance.

#

3. Birthing process

The first and most important thing that you need to do when your pig approaches the time of delivery is to keep her in a secluded barn or housing area. If not, you will have to look around for her all over the property. When pigs do not have a warm and quiet birthing area, they will find one themselves.

It is a challenge to look for the pig or heifer when she goes into reclusion on her own. It is also not the best thing to do to approach a pig who is trying to get some peace and quiet. With a barn where she is familiar with your movements, she will be much calmer.

Then, you will observe what stage of birthing she is in. If it is only the first stage, you will see her standing up and pacing around. They will lay down and get up several times.

If you can get close enough, you will see the water sac hanging from the birth canal. It will be yellowish in color. Usually, immediately after the appearance of this spherical sac, the feet of the piglet begin emerging.

The feet should be pointing towards the ground. If not, she is having a breached birth. Observe the pig after the feet start to emerge. If she is able to push the piglet out on her own, then it is best that you let her do so. If you see that after the feet have emerged, she has stayed in the same position for more than an hour, you may have to provide necessary assistance to pull the piglet out.

You may or may not have to restrain her. If the pig is sitting and settled, you should be able to pull the piglet out without any hassle. However, if she is standing and you are not sure if she is tame enough, you can restrain her for your own safety.

Using a head gate is the best possible option. If you do not have one, you can get a 10' gate to restrain her. The head gate is recommended as it will prevent any accident or damage if the pig begins to panic and decides to back onto you.

You will need a pair of shoulder gloves for hygiene purposes. Start by washing your hands from the shoulder to the fingertips. Then put the gloves on when your hands are fully dry.

It is necessary to apply some lubricant on the gloves to reach in and help pull the piglet out. You can try a vet recommended lubricant or can use petroleum jelly. You may have to reach into the birth canal to check on the position of the piglet.

Depending on the position of the piglet, you will be able to provide the right kind of assistance to the pig. Here are some positions that you can expect:

- **Backward position:** In this case, you do not have to turn the piglet around. You will have to wait until the hind legs of the piglet are presented before you provide any assistance. You will use a calving chain or any flexible rope that can be fastened to the piglet in order to pull it out as quickly as possible.

- **Breach position:** This is when the piglet is going to be born tail first. This is when you have to get the piglet into the correct position to avoid any complication. Push the piglet into the uterus as much as possible. The flexed hock will then be pushed away from the piglet. The fetlock on the foot should be pushed back inward. Hold the hock joints and the fetlock tight and bring the foot over the pelvic brim into the birth canal. This should be done for both the legs. After that you can tie the rope or the calving chain and begin to pull the piglet out.

- **Head down or head back position:** The piglet must be pushed back into the uterine cavity. With one hand, hold the piglet stable and cup the other one over the nose of the piglet. If you are unable to hold on to the head, you can even hook two fingers to the corner of the mouth to get a grip. Once you have hold of the piglet, you will turn him around to the normal position to make the birthing process simpler.

- **Foreleg back position:** The piglet will be pushed back in to the uterus. Then, grab the upper leg and pull the piglet forward enough to allow the knee to reach forward. Tightly flex the knee and pull forward. After you have flexed the knee tightly, you will cup the hoof with the hand and then bring it to a normal position.

- **Bent toe or caught elbow position:** The piglet should be pushed back into the uterine canal to adjust the position of the elbow and foot. If there is a caught elbow, you can grab the leg that is shoved further up and then pull it forward. As soon as you correct this, the piglet will come out quite easily.

Once the piglet is in the normal position that you can pull it out from, you can use a rope or a calving chain around the front leg of the piglet and then pull it out. It is best that you use a double half hitch knot.

You can put one loop on the fetlock and the other one just below the knee. When the pig is straining, you will pull. When the pig begins to rest, you need to stop pulling, too.

If a piglet puller is available to you, make use of it. It will help you prevent pulling the piglet out too quickly and causing damage. The piglet puller is a U-shaped part that is used on the rear of the pig to attach the chain and pull the piglet out. The puller is used at the base of the tail while the chain is attached to the legs of the piglet.

As you pull the piglet, you can tighten the rope of the chain enough to get the piglet out easily. When you feel that the tension is good enough to get the piglet out, you can work in the same rhythm as the contractions of the pig. Keep increasing the tension as needed to get a better grip.

At one point you will notice that the puller is no longer needed. This is usually when the piglet is half way out. Then you can unhook the chain and then pull the piglet out by hand.

As soon as the piglet is born, the first thing that you need to do is assist it to breathe. The nose should be cleaned out using your finger to get the amniotic fluid out. Follow this with a gentle tickle in the nose using a piece of hay.

You can also put a few drops of water in the ears to get the piglet to shake its head. In extreme cases, you will have to provide artificial respiration to make the piglet breathe. Ideally, a piglet should breathe within 60 seconds of being born.

The piglet should be shifted to a new pen which has clean straw as bedding. After that, you can let the mother enter the area and spend time with the little one.

The mother and the newborn piglet should be allowed to rest in a quiet area. The mother will lick the piglet clean and then persuade him to begin nursing. The mother pig needs a good amount of hay and clean water to relax after the strenuous birthing process.

Make sure that you keep her area clear of any disturbances such as a sudden sounds or even too much activity.

4. Mother and piglet behavior

Just between 2-5 hours after birth, suckling behavior starts as long as the mother is standing. The piglet will butt at the udder of the mother when he is learning to suckle. Heifers take more time to stand as the first birth is always difficult. Experienced pigs will stand up much faster.

In order to stimulate breathing, the mother will lick the piglet constantly. This simulates circulation and also excretion. It is common for the pig to hide the piglet as an instinct. This is to prevent predators from attacking the helpless young piglet. The pig will probably showcase this behavior even when she is on your farm.

Suckling begins with the front teat normally. It is most intense as soon as the piglet stands up. The piglet and the mother continue to increase the distance between them after calving. After some time, they will begin to communicate by vocalizing.

In the first week, the piglet will follow the pig. If you have a herd, you will notice that the piglets form a group of their own and stay in that group while the pigs graze. This group is called a nursery and is an indication that the piglets will begin to graze on their own soon.

You may even have a guard pig who will observe the behavior of the piglets in the initial period. Pigs are also ready to foster other piglets when they are nursing. The number of piglets that are nursed varies from one pig to the other.

When the pig is ready to give birth, she will seclude herself from the herd and will find a quiet place. If that is not possible, the herd will interfere, leading to a disruption in the bond between the mother and the piglet.

If you remove the piglets from the mother as soon as they are weaned, you can condition them better. This will help you get them used to human handling and will also be able to take care of procedures like dehorning, castration and others. They will be quieter and easier to handle as they age.

When they are constantly in contact with humans, they will be less stressed when they are expected to do so at a later age. If the piglet is left with the mother, they may be taught to avoid human interaction as a behavior. They will pick up other behavior as well that will make them hard to handle.

The mother pig uses the vocal, visual and olfactory senses to identify the piglet. When a pig begins to groom the piglet, she labels the piglet as her own. In most cases, the piglet will stand up in just 45 minutes of being born.

The mother will aid suckling by adjusting her body in a way that is easier for the little one to access. Until 7 months from being born, the suckling time of the piglet is about 34 minutes.

The frequency is between 4 to 5 times per day. Studies have revealed that heifers or female piglets are weaned at the age of 8 months while piglets are weaned at the age of 11 months.

The mother and the child should have a dry and soft surface to rest on. Then the piglet will be cleaned by the mother. If you find that she is licking the piglet for too long, it is good to separate the two so that the piglet has more time to nurse and feed with the mother. The hormonal activity in the body of the mother will determine her maternal behavior.

You cannot really predict maternal behavior in pigs, so one that makes a great mother may not necessary produce a heifer who has the same maternal behavior.

However, the bond between the mother and the piglet is quite strong. Within just five minutes of being born, the mother and the piglet will develop a specific maternal bond that helps the mother identify, nurture and protect her little one.

Sometimes, there can be abnormal maternal behavior that you need to have checked by a vet. If left unattended, such piglets may be in danger of being injured or staying malnourished as the mother refuses to feed them.

5. Abnormal breeding behavior

There are some behavioral patterns in the pig that you should watch out for. If the misbehavior is targeted towards the piglet, you must seek professional help. It may even help to find a foster for the newborn. Abnormal behavior includes:

- **Mismothering**: This is usually noticed in pigs that are in a very intensely managed maternity group. In most cases, in a very difficult birth that could have been long and painful, the mother will not stand up for suckling. Even the piglet may be too weak to suckle. Allowing an experienced pig to foster the piglet may work. If you do not have than option, hand feeding is the next best alternative.
- **Nymphomania:** Yes, it is possible for your livestock to exhibit this behavior. If the pig belongs to a breed, this behavior is more common. You will see that the pig begins to behave like a male pig. She will begin to paw and will mount other pigs or will simply not allow a piglet or another pig to mount her. She may even become aggressive. Nymphomania has been associated with cysts in the follicles.
- **Pigleter-steer syndrome:** If the pig is raised in an improper feedlot set up, she will display this health problem. This behavior tends to attract many pig who will mount the pig taking turns. This leads to serious injuries and the pigleter needs to be segregated from a herd. Almost 2% of the steers in a feedlot tend to display this health concern.
- **Illnesses**: If your livestock has any health issues, it will lead to abnormal behavior. A pig that is healthy will be alert at all times, will be vocal and will display behavior like stretching when they get up after a period of complete rest. But, an unwell pig will not move fast, will have dull eyes, will seem to be disinterested in the environment. They may also stop eating and nursing. There are several other indications of poor health including teeth grinding and

hunching the back. We will discuss this in detail in the following chapter.

There are options to normalize and modify this behavior through procedures like endocrine implants. It is also easier to handle livestock that has been neutered or spayed. If you are not interested in breeding your miniature pig, you can get them neutered at a young age to avoid these behaviors.

Normally, sexual behavior that is not ordinary is the result of endocrine imbalances, genetic issues and also poor management. The good news is that you can reverse most of this behavior with help from proper professionals.

It will also help to learn more about breeding behavior and general livestock behavior to make the environment less stressful for your pig.

Nutrition plays a big role in leading to good behavior. For instance, a piglet who is on a high protein diet will show more urge to masturbate.

In the breeding season, especially, the surge of hormones may lead to difficulty in handling your miniature pig. But with some patience and knowledge, you should be able to manage most situations effectively.

6. Raising piglets

Taking care of a newborn piglet is no piece of cake. You will require a lot of patience to make sure that the piglet is comfortable and is developing properly.

There are several reasons why you may have to take on this role. The mother may succumb to a difficult birthing process, she may develop abnormal behavior or you may just prefer to have a piglet that is hand raised. It is best that you handle the piglet after it has been weaned, but if you have to take care of a newborn piglet, here are a few tips and techniques.

Rearing a newborn piglet

If a newborn piglet has been orphaned, you will notice depression, dehydration and a loss of appetite. You will have to provide proper care for the first 24 hours to make sure that the piglet is healthy and to ensure survival.

Colostrum is needed for the newborn piglet in order to be healthy. This is the first milk that is produced by the mother. Passive immunity against possible health threats is provided with the colostrum, which is rich in minerals and vitamins.

In the first 36 hours of being born, it is necessary for the piglet to get this colostrum. You can either get it from the mother or can opt for artificial sources.

If you have several pigs in your herd that are calving, it is advised that you take one portion of the colostrum and freeze it. You can look for milk replacers that contain colostrum as well.

As soon as the piglet has consumed the colostrum, he can be given whole milk or a milk replacer. If you have frozen colostrum, you can hand feed the baby.

It should be warmed to 36 degrees before you feed it to the piglet. In case you have a good supply of colostrum available, you can feed it to the piglet for the first two days.

You must give him two feeds, one in the morning and one in the evening. Each portion should consist of at least 2 liters of colostrum for it to have the desired effect on the development of the piglet.

If the piglet is born dehydrated, you will have to rehydrate it before feeding. A piglet that is dehydrated will have scours or may not even survive if he is given milk before rehydration. You can make an electrolyte mixture at home or can purchase one from the vet.

At home, electrolytes can be made by adding ½ teaspoon of baking soda, 1 teaspoon of table salt and 125g of glucose to about 1.2 liters of water. Before you give the piglet any milk, make sure that he has received the electrolyte for at least 24 hours to rehydrate completely.

Feeding options

Livestock have four stomachs and are called ruminants. When the piglet is born, only the fourth stomach or the abomasum is the one that is functioning. It is harder to feed a piglet with teats but when the piglet suckles, the esophageal groove responds by closing and directing the milk directly to the fourth stomach where it is easily digested.

Using teats will also stimulate the production of saliva and will urge the piglet to take in more fluids. The teats should be kept clean at all times and if there is any deterioration in the condition of the teat, it must be replaced.

You have the option of using a bucket to feed the piglet as well, but the issue with the bucket is that the esophageal reflex is never triggered and the milk will go straight to the rumen.

The rumen is not functioning at this point and the milk stays undigested. This leads to scouring or diarrhea in the piglets.

When you use a bucket, you need to make sure that it is at least 30cms above the ground. This will help the groove close and prevent the milk from entering the rumen.

If your piglet does not take to the bucket instantly, you will have to train him to do so. Straddle the neck with the piglet backed into a corner. Moisten your fingers with milk and take it to the mouth of the piglet.

No matter what method you use, the piglet should be given a measured amount of milk. When the piglet gets older, he will begin to graze. Then, the other stomachs will begin to develop, so you need to make sure that your piglet has a good amount of high quality hay in order to stimulate the proper development of the rumen.

Controlling illnesses

One of the most common issues in young piglets is scouring or diarrhea. This can lead to death very quickly if not treated properly. When you notice this in a piglet, make sure that he is taken off milk for a minimum of four hours during which he is provided with a good amount of electrolytes.

In case scouring continues after this, you will need proper medication to help the piglet. This should be provided only after consulting the vet.

When you are expecting a piglet, keeping this scouring medicine handy can save the newborn's life. Make sure that the sick piglet is isolated.

You must always keep the environment of the piglet hygienic. If you are using teats, make sure that it is cleaned properly and is maintained in a good condition. This is one of the best ways to prevent any illness in hand raised piglets.

The piglet must always have ample water to drink. This will keep them healthy. Piglets will not drink any water up to two weeks of age. By the time they are six weeks old, they will be consuming almost five liters of water each day. You cannot expect water to be replaced with milk even if you are feeding the piglet twice a day.

The water bowl needs to be cleaned regularly as the piglet may foul it while feeding. You must also allow the piglet to interact with older ones that have a fully developed rumen. This will help them pick up some necessary microbes that aid digestion of food in the rumen.

They are passed on from one piglet to the other when they graze on the same pasture. They can also be spread through behavior like licking, which is very common when piglets are being introduced to one another, almost like an approval.

How to make a piglet feeding program successful

- If you are using milk replacers, make sure that they contain 10% fat, 20% protein and not more than 10% of starch and sugar. Reconstitute the feed and provide it as per the instructions given by the manufacturer.

- You can increase the portion of the powder if you are feeding the piglets only once in order to reduce the volume of food required.

- If you are feeding more than one piglet, you will draft them as per the feeding habit.

- Milk should be divided into separate feeds. One can be given in the morning and the other in the evening at a regular time.

- As the piglet grows and begins to forage, you can give him one feed a day. Make sure that he has a lot of cool and fresh water to drink at this stage.

- Good hygiene is a must when you are hand-raising a piglet.

- You must never over fed a piglet. This is especially important in the first three weeks of their life, as it may lead to diarrhea or scouring. You must feed a piglet 10% of his body weight every day. For example, if the piglet weighs about 20 kilos you will provide 2 L of milk every day.

- The milk should be at a temperature between 35 to 38 degrees.

- Clean water should be provided at all times. The water trough should be cleaned out regularly to prevent the chance of any diseases.

- You must never alter the amount of feed that you are giving the piglet suddenly.

- As piglets get older, they will need more food. Milk replacer is an expensive option. It is a better idea to make up for the required volume of food with grain and pellet.

- You can make this available at all times. They will feed on their own and will slowly increase the amount of grain that they consume. This will make it a lot easier for you to wean the piglet when the time comes.

- When you switch to solid foods, make sure that good quality hay is introduced along with concentrates when the piglet is about two weeks old.

Weaning a piglet

- You can wean a piglet more easily at a younger age. Providing milk up to 12 weeks of age is good enough as long as the piglet is in good health and is developing properly.

- If you introduce grains and solid food when the piglet is about one week old, you will be able to wean him off milk completely by the time he is five weeks old.

- You must wean the piglet as per the consumption of concentrate. When the piglet is consuming at least 650 g in a day you should feed wean them.

- Do not use age as a basis to wean the piglet. In some cases, the piglet will be able to reach this target earlier.

- You can reduce the milk concentration over a week to make weaning quicker and more abrupt.

- You will have to provide the weaned piglet with good management. Otherwise, poor nutrition and poor management will lead to stunted growth that cannot be reversed.

- In the case of young piglets, the diet should contain at least 20% of crude proteins.

- Make sure you provide fresh feed every day and clean out any leftovers from the trough every time you feed.

Providing solid food

- When the piglet is about one week old, you can start by providing access to clean hay all day.

- This will improve the activity of the rumen. By the time the piglet is about 12 weeks old, the rumen should be functioning normally.

- You will only give them high quality baby piglet meal or good quality pellets until they are about five weeks old.

- Green grass in excess should be avoided until the piglet is 6 weeks old to prevent any indigestion.

- You can provide concentrates to the pig by adding a little to the milking bucket. Just when the piglet is about to finish drinking the milk, you can rub some concentrate on the muzzle. This will encourage them to taste it.

- By the time the piglet is three weeks old, you can give him meals hay, grain and access to green pasture in small amounts. Any change that you make in the feed should be gradual.

- As per the quality of the pasture, you may have to provide the piglet with concentrates and supplementary hay until the piglet reaches the desired body weight.

- The concentrate that you provide to your piglet should have a coarse texture, should be highly palatable and should provide the piglet with proteins, roughage and a lot of energy.

- A good mix includes four parts crushed grain and one part linseed, peanut, cottonseed meal or copra. You can also add a small amount of molasses to it to make the piglet relish it more.

- You can add rumen modifiers as advised by the vet. This will improve the activity of the rumen and will also prevent any chances of coccidiosis in piglets.

- You can add this as per the instructions of the manufacturer. It can be added to pellets, molasses based food mix and also pre-mixed meals. You must not add it to any urea based supplement.

- Rumen modifiers should be provided in small quantities as an excess can be toxic.

- You can provide protein meals as a natural source of bypass and rumen degradable proteins.

- You must never provide non protein sources of nitrogen such as urea when the piglet is very young.

- The best hay for young piglet is Lucerne hay. It should be checked for any weed or mold before feeding it to the piglets.

- If you have a pasture that is scarce or is not of good quality, supplementing the feed with good quality hay will work wonders.

As discussed, rearing and hand raising piglets can be a difficult task. The goal must always be healthy development of your pet and if you have any queries, you can speak to your vet for more suggestions.

Chapter 6: Dietary requirements of the micro pig

As the owner or as the prospective owner of a micro pig, it should be your foremost concern to provide adequate and proper nutrition to the pet. If the pet animal deficient in any nutrient, he will develop various deficiencies and acquire many diseases. When the nutrition is right, you can easily ward off many dangerous diseases.

Each animal species is different. Just because certain kinds of foods are good for your pet dog, it does not mean that they will be good for your pet micro pig also. It is important to learn about all the foods that the micro pigs are naturally inclined to eating. You should always be looking at maintaining good health of your pet.

It is important to learn about the foods that are good for your micro pig, however you should also understand that the foods that you feed your pet with could be lacking in certain nutrients. An animal in the wild is different from one in captivity. The availability of certain foods will also affect the diet of your pet.

Generally, the food given to captive pets is lacking in certain nutrients. If such is the case, you will have to give commercial pellets to your micro pig. These pellets are known to compensate for the various nutritional deficiencies that the animal might have due to malnutrition.

You should always aim at providing wholesome nutrition to your pet. It is important to understand the pet's nutritional requirements and include all the nutrients in his daily meals. To meet his nutritional requirements, you might also have to give him certain supplements.

The supplements will help you to make up for the essential nutrients that are not found in his daily meals. Though these supplements are easily available, you should definitely consult a veterinarian before you give your micro pig any kind of supplements.

It is very important that you serve only high quality food to your pet. If you are trying to save some money by buying cheaper, low quality alternatives, then you are in a bad situation. A low quality food will affect the health of the micro pig.

You can expect him to acquire deficiencies and diseases when he is not fed good quality food. The cure is taking the pet to the veterinarian. This in turn will only cost you more money. To avoid this endless loop, it is better to work on the basics. Keep the pet healthy by feeding him with high quality food, rather than spending money on him by taking him to the veterinarian.

Maintaining the health of your livestock comes from good husbandry and care. There are a few things that form the basics of proper livestock care and you need to ensure that you take care of everything to keep your heard safe and healthy.

Here are some tips to provide best possible care to your beloved miniature livestock.

1. Feeding miniature livestock

While the type of food required by mini and regular sized livestock is practically the same, the quantity is what matters. Now, a rule of thumb is that a pig or piglet will consume his own body weight's equivalent over the month. So if your pig is 50lb, he will need 50lb of feed every month.

You need to make sure that your pig gets all the nutrients required for proper growth and development. It is not as simple as just placing a stack of hay in front of the pig. You need to investigate the requirements of your livestock and understand what is required to fulfill the nutritional requirements. You may have to provide different types of feed to meet the nutritional requirements of your miniature livestock.

The forage quality is of great importance. If you are unsure about the ration formulation, you can even consult a breeder or your vet to provide you with tips. The livestock needs to be assessed to understand the requirement completely.

Assessing livestock

You have to first assess the requirements of your livestock to make sure that they are getting what their body demands. Here are a few factors that you must consider:

- **The environment of the animals:** Depending on what is naturally available to these animals in their local environment, you can prepare a nutritious meal plan for them. The local environment also affects the demands and the water requirement of each.

- **The productivity status of the livestock:** You can divide livestock into various classes based on the growth, lactation and reproduction as well as other categories including the gender, breed, fat level, weight and the amount of weight gain or loss required. Based on this you can formulate a ration for your miniature livestock.

- **The current climatic conditions:** The climatic changes affect the animal based on the thickness of the hide, the hair condition and the depth of the hair.

There are two options when it comes to feeding your livestock. You can stick to dry lot feeding where the food is harvested and stored before giving it to your livestock. The next option is to let the livestock graze if you have a large enough pasture.

With dry-lot livestock, if you are unable to offer a bedding of straw or sawdust and provide mud instead, it will affect the level of consumption to a large extent. However, the nutrition requirements should be kept in mind irrespective of the kind of feed you offer.

2. What to feed your livestock

If you provide your livestock with only a grain mix or grain feed, the feeding technique is called feed-lotting. Essentially, livestock are anatomically designed to consume grass or roughage. Grain feeding involves providing livestock with a certain ration that consists of a mix of different grains.

For a balanced meal, it is a good idea to allow the animals to graze at least once a day and then provide them with a grain mix or hay and alfalfa grass.

While nutritionally, grass feeding and grain feeding will not have too much difference, the latter makes the livestock stressed as it is far removed from their normal biological need. Therefore, a mix or adding supplements to grazing livestock is recommended.

Avoid hay as a substitute for grazing. Naturally, hay makes for less than 10% of the diet of livestock. Confined grain feeding is usually directed towards helping the livestock grow fast. This is a practice followed in show animals as well as in animals that are mainly reared for meat.

Essentially, a grain mix consists of a mixture of Soy hull, molasses, whole oats, cracked corn, canola mean and a Vitamin B1 supplement. You can also add some calcium carbonate to this mixture to make your livestock's digestive system healthier and to prevent any bloating.

Livestock require trace minerals in small amounts. There are two types of minerals you need to provide: macro minerals and micro minerals. The former is required in higher levels than the latter.

Micro minerals will improve healthy hooves, hair and skin and will also boost the immune system of your livestock. If you are only grass feeding your livestock, you can add recommended supplements to fulfill the mineral requirements. Make sure you consult your vet before giving your livestock any form of supplements.

For grass fed livestock, they will need at least half an acre per head. If this is not available, you can provide fresh alfalfa grass as a substitute.

One of the most important nutrients for any animal is water. They need water in order to digest and absorb the nutrients that you are providing with the diet. In the colder and warmer months, make sure to check that the temperature of the water remains at room temperature. You may have to shift to large water troughs if you have a natural source that gets to hot or perhaps freezes over in winters.

Now, you can feed livestock twice a day. Keep the feeding time consistent and make sure that there is a gap of 12 hours between each feed. During the summers, appetite will decrease and it will help to provide the first feed earlier in the morning. You also must make sure that the livestock is eating well. Ideally, the food that you provide should be consumed within 30 minutes, indicating a healthy eating habit.

3. Ideal feeding routine

Good nutrition is the key to preventing several diseases. You need to have a feeding management practice or a proper routine that will help you do the same.

Most hoof related diseases that are a major concern for livestock are related to the feeding frequency and the size of the forages and grains. If you are transitioning your miniature pig to a new diet, putting them into a routine can be one of the key factors in determining health.

If you have a herd, you must give them a grain mix twice each day. If your pig is milking, you can even increase it to three or four portions as recommended by your vet. This should be followed by foraging on a pasture for at least an hour.

If you are giving your livestock only mixed rations, make sure that you check all the high moisture food thoroughly. These herds must be checked every quarter to ensure that they are getting all the nutrients that are required for them. Make sure that you keep the mix consistent and balanced. Providing grains outside the regular mix means that your pigs will begin to have preferences for what they want to eat.

You can also include dietary buffers. You will have to add about 0.8% of the dry matter equivalent to the diet. These buffers will prevent any acidosis in the rumen of your livestock.

The particle size of the forage and the grain is also of great importance. If the particle size in your grain mix or forage is too small and the amount of fiber provided is low, they can lead to serious health issues. You need to distribute the feed and the forage particles in a way that the pigs are able to digest properly.

The processing method of the grains and the moisture content in the food also chances the availability of non-fiber carbohydrates. This is a major concern when you do not provide forage with a grain mix.

If you are switching any animal from one diet to another, you need to keep the transition as gradual as possible. For example, when you are changing the diet of a calving pig, you can increase the concentrate of feed to about 0.75 percent of the body weight. Ideally, the animals that are on one type of diet should be divided into a different group with an entirely different ration.

With a smaller body weight, you need to be careful with the portion that you provide your pig with. The nutrients should be balanced. In order to develop properly, pigs require vitamins, trace minerals, proteins and carbohydrates. If you are unsure of how to achieve this balance, it is best that you consult your vet.

You may change the routine slightly with weather changes. Even this should be done gradually to prevent any stress to the animal. Stress always compromises the immune system and provides a gateway for several disease causing microbes.

4. Supplements

The diet of the micro pig should be highly nutritious. If you make sure that the micro pig is getting all its necessary nutrients from the food itself, you can avoid the use of supplements. At times, your micro pig's diet might not be able to provide it with the right set of nutrients and vitamins. In such a case, it becomes necessary to introduce supplements in the diet of the micro pig.

If the pet is not well and is recuperating from an injury or disease, the veterinarian might advise you to administer certain supplements to the pet. These supplements will help the pet to heal faster and get back on his feet sooner.

You should always consult a veterinarian before you give any supplement to the micro pig. He/she will be the best judge of which supplements the micro pig requires and which ones he doesn't.

There are many vitamin supplements that are available in tasty treat forms for the micro pig. While you can be sure that your pet is getting the right nutrients, the pet can enjoy the treat given to him.

You can also include supplements of fatty acids in the diet of the micro pig. A few drops of this kind of supplement will enhance the taste and the nutritional value of the food item that is being served to the micro pig.

While it can be necessary to supplement certain vitamins and nutrients to the pet, you should also be aware of the hazards of over feeding a certain nutrient. If there is an overdose of a certain vitamin in the body of the micro pig, it can lead to vitamin toxicity.

Another point that you should take care of is that you should not blindly follow the instructions and dosage that is printed on various supplements. The food that you feed the micro pig will also have a supply of vitamins. The micro pig will only require some extra dosage.

5. Switching foods

It would take you time to understand the diet preferences of the new pig. Miniature pigs form their preferences quite early in their lives.

This means that the first six months is a great time for you to introduce different kinds of foods to the miniature pig. This will help him to have his preferences and will also make things easier for you. If your miniature pig likes three kinds of food items instead of one, it gets easier for you also.

In case a certain food item is not available, you know that you have other choices. If you don't introduce new foods to the miniature pig, he will turn out to be very fussy. In addition, you the parent will have a hard time keeping the taste buds happy.

If you want to introduce new foods or switch foods, you can't suddenly change his usual meal plan. This will put off the miniature pig. There are some simple tips and tricks that you should be following to make sure that the pet is eating well even when new foods are being introduced.

A simple way of introducing new food in the diet of the miniature pig is by starting out with a small amount of the food. Take a bowl and add the usual food of the pet in it. Now, take a very small amount of the new food that you wish to feed your pet in the bowl. Mix the contents and serve the food to the miniature pig.

Just keep adding a very small amount of the food item in the usual food of the pet. Initially, the miniature pig will get used to the smell of the new food. This might take some time, so be prepared. Once you see that the pet miniature pig has started eating the new food along with the usual old food, you can gradually increase the portion of the new food and decrease the portion of the old food.

The given process will take some days, but you will have to have some patience. The idea is to help the miniature pig get used to the scent of a food before you can expect the pet to eat the food. Once he is okay with the scent, he will try out the food item on his own.

If you are looking for another trick to introduce a new food item and switch between food items, then here is another one for you. Take some water in a bowl and add the two food items in the bowl. You can keep the quantity of the old food item a little more than the new one. Now, just stir this mixture and heat it for some time.

Don't heat the mixture of the food items for too long. You just need to heat it for seconds so that the smells blend with one another. This trick is also useful when the miniature pig is sick and is refusing to eat anything.

A point that should be noted here is that you should throw away the contents of the bowl that your pet does not eat. Don't keep it to serve him in the next meal. This is because the kibble gravy and water will cause the food items to spoil if they are kept for too long.

Chapter 7: Health of the micro pig

An unhealthy pet can be a nightmare for any owner. The last thing that you would want is to see your pet in pain. Many disease causing parasites dwell in unhygienic places and food. If you take care of the hygiene and food of the micro pig, there are many diseases that you can avert.

At times, even after all the precautions that you take, the pet can get sick. It is always better to be well equipped so that you can help your pet. You should always consult a vet when you find any unusual traits and symptoms in the pet.

You should understand the various health related issues that your pet micro pig can suffer from. This knowledge will help you to get the right treatment at the right time. It is also important that you understand how you can take care of a sick pet. This knowledge will help you to keep your calm and help the sick micro pig.

Maintaining your miniature pig includes proper care and food. Above all, you need to make sure that your pig is free from any illnesses. You need to be extra cautious, as there are several bovine diseases that can also be transmitted to humans through milk or through the environment.

From finding a reliable vet to having a proper program to prevent common illnesses, this chapter will take you through all the aspects of perfect healthcare that you need to provide to your mini.

1. Identifying illness in miniature pigs

Providing timely assistance is key to maintaining your miniature livestock. Only when you are able to identify a possible illness will you be able to provide the right medication at the right time. Be observant of your mini and make sure that you note down any deviation from normalcy. Here are some definite signs that your livestock will display when sick or injured.

Check the body temperature

If you keep regular tabs on the temperature of the pig's body, you will be able to identify an illness almost immediately. In several piglets, the best indication of illness is body temperature, as they otherwise provide very little or confusing visual signs.

The rule of thumb is that any increase in temperature above 104 degrees Fahrenheit in rectal temperature is a sign of illness. Of course, you must never neglect visual signs irrespective of the body temperature of the pig.

The body responds in the most natural manner to disease causing organisms. The immune system prepares to fight the infection, thus causing a temperature surge. In some cases, the pig will be able to overcome the infection on their own and will recover without any signs.

In other cases, you will have a noticeable increase in body temperature along with other visual signs. Neglecting this will lead to the worsening of clinical signs and may lead to death if the pig is not treated.

The earlier you detect an elevation in body temperature, the more effective treatment is.

The biggest problem that you will face with livestock is that there is no "normal" body temperature per say. The body temperature is low in the morning and continues to raise throughout the day. This heat load is shed fast as nighttime approaches, enough to reach a minimum temperature in the morning. This fluctuation of body temperature occurs even in the colder months.

During daylight hours, the temperature will increase even when the temperature of the environment is controlled and maintained at a standard, so it is clear that only the environment does not affect the body temperature of pigs.

There are several factors like the level of activity, feeding, humidity and solar radiation that affect the body temperature of pigs. You will see rapid increase in body temperature after the pig has eaten or after any exercise.

This is the primary reason why livestock must be allowed ample rest after sundown. While it may seem like a good time to take them out to the field, they have to rest in order to let go of the body heat. This is especially true when the day is very hot.

On warm days, it is critical to note the body temperature of the pig in the afternoon. Many farm owners will allow the livestock to rest or just stand for about three hours before they measure the body temperature in the afternoons.

You must also follow this procedure to minimize any form of stress before you take the body temperature.

Visual signs of illness

Loss of appetite is the first give away of illness in pigs. When a pig is exposed to any respiratory disease, his appetite will begin to decrease in just 48 hours from infection. This is much before an elevation in body temperature is noticed.

Make sure that you observe your livestock whenever you feed them. You cannot really monitor them when they are grazing on a daily basis. However, you can make up for that by checking the gut fill of the pig.

If the belly is bouncing as he walks and the pig looks gaunt, it is a sign that he may not be eating as well. He may have also stopped consuming water in the required quantity. If the body condition deteriorates and the weight reduces rapidly, it is an indication of illness.

There are other signs that you need to watch out for including:

- Deep coughing

- Depression

- Drooping head and ears

- Slow movement

- Lagging behind when in a herd

- Reluctance to stand up

- Nasal discharge

- Eye discharge

- Bloody diarrhea

These symptoms are noticed after the animal has stopped feeding properly and after the rectal temperature is high. Therefore, the more you observe your livestock, the faster will you be able to get them the treatment that they need in order to fight an infection.

Sometimes, the signs of illnesses can even be caused by a vaccination provided to the pig. When you put your pig on any vaccination program, be sure to check with the vet about the possible symptoms that you can expect.

That way you will be able to distinguish if the pig is actually ill or whether he is experiencing a temporary side effect caused by the vaccination.

Livestock manure can also be examined to determine whether your pig is sick or not. If the manure is loose and has large particles of feed along with blood and mucus, it can indicate some sort of injury. In the case of a grazing herd, you cannot really separate the specific pig or piglet. Then, an abnormality in the manure is a sign for you to become alert and keep an eye on the herd. It is common for a pig to defecate when being handled. Make sure that you keep an eye out for any abnormality when you are doing so.

Identifying injuries

The injuries in livestock can range from minor to severe. Sometimes, it is easy to detect the injury upon observation. These injuries usually manifest in the form of lameness or inability to stand up. With such injuries, it becomes hard to sell a pig. Besides that, you do not have to worry about the general behavior of your pet after she has been treated.

There are other injuries that have more subtle signs and symptoms. These include bruises and any form of organ damage that can be caused by diseases like hardware disease. You can expect such an injury if the animal shows sudden changes in appetite and becomes reluctant to move.

You must examine the immediate environment of the pig to make sure that there aren't any potential hazards that could have led to an injury. The horns of other animals in the herd can also cause a significant amount of bruising. This is most common during breeding season or if you are not providing enough food, leading to competition within the herd. If there are any sharp objects such as nails in the handling area and the pastures, they may injure the pig as well.

The key to treating injuries is to observe the animal when you are feeding them or washing them. You can check for any mild lacerations or cuts, blood vessel ruptures, mouth injuries, foot injuries, eye injuries or any damage caused by insect bites. In order to notice these injuries, you will have to make sure that you pay close attention whenever you are handling the animal.

In most cases, this can be treated in your home while keeping the pig restrained. If you are unsure of the type of injury and the treatment, you may have to contact your vet immediately to check the pig.

When you notice that your pet is sick or injured, it should be managed immediately. It is very common for livestock to be put down, on large farms, because the initial symptoms were ignored. You certainly do not want that for your beloved pet mini.

Work with your vet to figure out a program or a routine that can keep the health of your mini in top shape. If there are any situations that are not included in the plan, you can contact your vet for any assistance. The more you learn about livestock health, the better you will be able to prevent diseases and illnesses in your pet.

2. Common health issues

There are a few diseases that your miniature pig is prone to. If you have raised a regular sized stock, the diseases that affect them will affect a miniature pig as well. Here are some diseases that you must look out for:

Tick borne diseases

- The damage caused by ticks is mostly around the ear and udder area. These wounds tend to get infected and will eventually be attacked by flies.

- Certain ticks like the ones that cause heart water infection tend to cause more damage in livestock than other types of ticks.

- Treating for ticks is necessary every week during the rainy season and every fortnight during the dry season.

- If the pig is vaccinated, then you will be able to treat them less often and still prevent tick borne diseases.

- Ticks will infect livestock with several diseases like gall sickness.

- European breeds tend to be at a greater risk of getting these diseases.

- The older the animal, the greater the risk of tick borne diseases.

- Vaccination and other preventive measures can be taken against tick borne diseases.

- It is best that you have the piglet vaccinated before the age of 6 months to make sure that they stay free from tick borne diseases.

Redwater disease

- Redwater is accompanied by symptoms like:

  - Red urine

  - Pale and yellow gums

  - Pale eyes

  - Loss of appetite

  - Nervous signs such as inability to walk.

- The pig may succumb to this condition if not treated appropriately and in time.

- Keeping the livestock free from any stress is a big part of the treatment program. Make sure that you do not graze them over long distances

- It is advised to inject them with Imizol or Berenil.

Heartwater

- The most common signs are:

  - Depression

  - Fever

  - High stepping

  - Convulsions

- When left untreated, death is inevitable with your miniature pig if he is infected with heartwater.

- The best possible treatment is tetracycline.

- With tick borne diseases, proper hygiene and timely care is the best way to prevent any complications. You must also control the insects in the housing area to prevent diseases from spreading from the infected animal to the others. It is a good idea to isolate any pig who has severe tick infestation.

Tuberculosis

- Sudden weight loss is the most sure shot indication of tuberculosis in livestock.

- A simple skin test can be done every year by the state vet to check if your pig has tuberculosis.

- When an animal is tested positive for tuberculosis, he will be given a T-brand on the neck.

Livestock measles

- This is a type of measles that is caused by tapeworm in livestock. It can infect people only when the meat of an infected animal is consumed.

- Usually livestock will pick up tapeworm eggs when they are grazing. The cause for infestation of the pasture is due to poor toilet practices by people in some areas.

- The measles is not visible in the animal and is normally seen only when the meat is cut.

- Proper hygiene is necessary to keep the animals free from tapeworm infection.

Anthrax

- This disease can lead to sudden death in livestock.

- People catch the infection when they consume the meat and also through cuts and sores on the animal's body.

- If an animal has succumbed to this disease, it is best to bury or burn the carcass.

- The only way to prevent the condition is with proper vaccination.

- If your pig has anthrax they will experience:

  - Nausea

  - Loss of appetite

  - Vomiting

  - Fever

  - Diarrhea

  - Vomiting blood

- In case you have any suspicion of an anthrax infection, you may want to check with your state vet.

Rabies

- This is not a very common condition in livestock but an infection can be caused if the pig is bitten by a rabid dog or jackal.

- The livestock will either be too excited and aggressive or will seem like he has no energy at all.

- If you reach into the pig's mouth for a routine dental examination or if you are bitten by a pig with rabies, you can be infected.

- It is only possible to vaccinate a pig against rabies as there is no cure once the animal has been infected.

Foot related problems

The hoof is one of the most sensitive areas of your pig's body. It is the area that comes into contact with moisture and dirt and when not maintained well, can get seriously infected. Some of the most common foot related issues are:

Laminitis

This is when the dermal layers of the feet have an aseptic inflammation. This leads to sensitivity and inflammation. The symptoms of the condition are:

- Diarrhea

- Moving in a stiff and cramped manner

- Standing on the toes while moving to the very edge of the stall to reduce pain

- Hemmorrhages in the sole

- Yellow coloration of the sole.

- A white line may appear in the junction between the sole and the wall of the hoof.

- Cracked heels

- Double soles

Sometimes the animal may not show any sign of lameness or pain. While you cannot point out to one causal factor, some of the most significant reasons include:

- Increased fermented carbohydrates leading to acidosis of the rumen.

- Poor nutritional management.

- Hormonal changes during parturition or the lactation cycle.

- Digestive or metabolic disorders.

- Infections such as foot rot, meritis and mastitis.

- Hard surfaces in the housing area.

- Lack of proper bedding.

- Overstraining of the body.

- Undesirable walking surface.

Rumen acidosis

- This is one of the primary contributing factors to lamintis.

- It is caused by the ingestion of more carbohydrates than the rumen can ferment.

- Fiber digestion is reduced and the production of lactic acid increases.

- When the amount of fermentable carbohydrates in the food increases, the amount of rumen bacteria also goes up, producing a lot of fatty acids.

- Eventually, the pH of the rumen reduces affecting the bacterial population negatively, leading them to diminish.

- When pH is below 5, the amount of lactic acid produced increases. This leads to acidosis.

- This, in turn, triggers the release of several endotoxins that leads to histamine release.

- Eventually, the lamina is destroyed, hoof deteriorates and laminitis occurs.

- Histamine is normally released when the pig is stressed, so it is possible that even environmental stress and an infection may lead to rumen acidosis.

Acute laminitis

- Systemic illness is noticed in the case of acute laminitis.

- The corium is very evidently inflamed.

- The condition may recur if the metabolism rate is not restored.

- Swelling and an increase in body temperature is the first sign of acute laminitis.

- You will also notice a coronary band in the area that consists of the soft tissue.

Subclinical laminitis

- Inflammation leads to hemorrhaging eventually.

- The horn tissue grows and the hemorrhage moves quickly to the surface.

- The sole is normally 0.4 inches thick. As the hemorrhage rises, the thickness increases by 0.2 inches each month.

- This is why the hemorrhage is only noticed about two months after the infection.

- If you notice these sole hemorrhages and any yellow coloration of the hoof, the condition could be rampant in the herd.

Other diseases

There are several other diseases that affect pigs particularly. Here are a few that you will have to watch out for in order to keep your pet safe from any chance of infection.

Respiratory diseases

- Also known as shipping fever, this is a type of pneumonia that is caused when the piglets have been shipped.

- There are several other factors that can lead to this condition.

- Stress related to weaning, weather changes and shipping will make the pig susceptible to these infections.

- It is natural for the pig to feel some stress when they are made to travel. However, this can be managed by handling them carefully and keeping the conditions within the shipping vehicle sanitary.

- Vaccination is the best preventive measure against this condition.

- Make sure that the piglet is vaccinated when he is very young. If not, they will not be able to survive should they contract this disease.

Backleg disease

- The medical term for this condition is clostridial disease.

- While there are over 60 strains of clostridial bacteria, not all of them will cause the condition in pigs.

- This condition is more common in pigs that are younger than 2 years of age. A gangrene formed in the muscle is the main reason for this infection.

- When the young piglet does not get ample colostrum, this disease may occur.

- In older livestock, it is the result of the contamination of the vaccination needle.

Bovine respiratory syncytial virus

- This condition can be fatal in livestock at times.

- It is normally caused due to stress and may lead to severe diseases of the respiratory system.

- It will also compromise the immunity of the animal against several other diseases.

- The common symptoms include high fever and a runny nose.

Viral Diarrhea

- This is one of the most expensive diseases contracted by livestock.

- The common signs are nasal discharge, fever, coughing and scurs.

- The more severe form of this disease is known as Type 2 Bovine Viral Diarrhea.

- It leads to hemorrhaging in young piglets and can also lead to severe infections in the adults.

Rhinotracheitis

- This is a mild respiratory disease that often compromises the immunity of the animal.

- It is dangerous, as it opens up the possibility of several other infections and diseases.

- The virus is shed through discharge in the eyes and the nose.

- In non-vaccinated animals, infections can be caused through the nasal passage and the mouth.

Haemophilus Somnus

- This is a type of bacterial infection that can lead to a series of neurological, reproductive and respiratory diseases in the pig.

- The common signs are rapid breathing, inflammation of the nasal passage, deep cough and a loss of appetite.

The best thing about pigs is that they can heal wonderfully when you provide them with the right type of care and medical attention. The best way to control any infection in your pet and within your herd, if you have one, is to practice good husbandry and provide the animal with a stress free environment.

3. Finding the right vet

When you bring a miniature pig home, the first thing that you need to do is look for a vet. Do not wait until there is an emergency to look for one. The thing with livestock is that the vet should be specialized to deal with farm animals. There are fewer specialized vets who are already working with a large base of farms, so looking for one near you and one who is conveniently accessible is a challenge.

Besides finding a vet, it is good for you to build a good rapport with your vet before you actually bring your mini home.

If your vet is familiar with your property and farm area, he will be able to make better recommendations to get your miniature pig into an effective healthcare regimen. They will also be able to come over in case of any emergency after your pet has been transported from the breeder to your home.

In areas where there aren't too many farms, it is harder to find a livestock vet. As for the vets that are available, it is possible that they are already taking care of a large part of the livestock in that area. So, the earlier you build a rapport, the easier it will be to seek assistance when it is really needed.

Even if the vet is unable to visit the animal, he or she will be able to give you the necessary advice on the phone in case of an emergency. Of course, the better the relationship, the more you can count on getting the right assistance even if it is in the middle of the night.

There are a few reliable sources that you can choose to get recommendations for a local livestock vet. To begin with, you can check with the Cooperative Extension office in your area where you normally purchase food and other supplies for your pet.

They can recommend specialized vets and also one who will be willing to visit your farm when needed. You can call the Cooperative extension office and ask them for the current list of veterinarians.

Alternatively, you can even check the website of the USDA or its counterpart in other countries for a list of the closest extension office so that you can get all the information that you need on livestock vets.

There are several other experts who can help you with healthcare for your beloved pet. For instance, in a cooperative office, you should be able to find nutrition specialists. They can also give you some technical assistance when needed.

The other reliable source to get leads into local livestock vets is another farm owner. It does not matter if they own a mini or not. They will definitely be able to get you in touch with a vet who takes care of their livestock. This may include goats, chickens or any other farm animal or bird. Word of mouth is, in fact, the most reliable source.

You can also look for information on the websites of veterinary associations such as:

- The American Association of Small Ruminant Practitioners

- The American Association of Bovine Practitioners

- The American Association of Swine Veterinarians

- American College of Veterinary Surgeons

- American College of Veterinary Internal Medicine

If you live near a state university or college that has a veterinary division, you can also check with them for leads. In some cases they may have a hospital and clinic in house that will work perfectly in case of an emergency. Some specialists will also make farm visits when necessary provided you are within a limited distance from the clinic.

When you are looking for a vet, there are some characteristics that will make you work well with your vet.

- The vet follows the same ideals that you do when it comes to raising your mini.

- Of course, you have to be flexible in your values, yet there are some factors that cannot change. For instance if you prefer to grass feed your mini, your vet must also be in favor of it.

- However, there may be times when you and your vet may not have the same logic or ideals. That is alright as long as they are respectful of your principles and are willing to work around it.

- When it comes to the welfare of your pet, you must also be willing to accept some advice from the vet even if it is not exactly what you believe in. For example, in some cases, you may have to switch to grain feed for an antibiotic to work better.

- In these cases, you can ask your vet why a certain method is better than the other. This will give you extra knowledge about your mini as well.

Once you have found a vet who is conveniently located and is comfortable to work with, you can ask the following questions to be entirely sure of the choice you make:

- What are your working hours?

- What equipment and livestock diagnostic resources are available with you?

- Are you available for emergencies?

- In case of an emergency, if the vet is not available, who will cover for them?

- What are the payment options?

- What is the regular fee per visit?

- Is there an additional charge to make a farm visit? If so, what are the charges?

- How can one contact the vet in case of an emergency?

There are several tips that you can take from your vet to provide first aid in case of an emergency. However, when the condition is serious, you should be able to call your vet who has all the skills to restore the health of your pig.

4. Preventive care

With the severity of infection in miniature pigs and the rapid onset of the condition, there is no option but to take all the preventive measures possible to ensure that your pet is safe and in perfect health.

The first step is to make sure that disease resistance is high in your mini. This can be taken care of with good nutrition and plenty of fresh and clean water. Livestock rely extensively on the pasture that they graze on for food as well as shelter. You will have to constantly keep a check on the quality and the quantity of grass available in your pasture.

The more important thing is to make sure that you keep the grazing area free from any debris. Sadly, people tend to throw food wrappers, drink cans and bottles out in open areas without a second thought. If any of this garbage blows into the pasture, you pig may end up eating it. As discussed, the blockage is only surgically manageable.

It is a good idea to walk the line of the fence every day to check for loose wires, any debris and also to check the safety of the fence that you have put up.

Vaccination is a must against all major diseases such as anthrax. You can contact your vet for a list of vaccines that are recommended for your miniature. You can also contact the cooperative extension in your area to find out what vaccination is necessary for any localized illness.

The vaccination schedule must be accurate and you need to ensure that you always get the boosters on time. Worming is also recommended to prevent several health issues in your pig.

You can obtain a computerized system that will help you maintain records and track your herd health on a schedule. You can check the weight and even figures like the sale price of a certain member of your herd. When you want to change the composition of a herd or want to include a new member, these programs will give you a lot of data.

You must also invest in proper handling material such as harnesses and also proper transport to ensure that there is no hassle when you have to make a routine visit to the vet or when your vet comes over for a checkup.

There are two aspects of preventive care: Pasture management and herd management. Here are some tips that will help you take care of each one correctly.

Pasture management

- Plant the area with nutritious varieties of grass on a regular basis. This will keep the grazing composition balanced. You can mix rye, white clover, fescue, orchard grass and other types of forage grass.

- You must be able to identify all the poisonous plans in your area to make sure that they do not grow in the area. A proper program should be created to eradicate any toxic plant.

- Pasture rotation is a good idea if you have room. When you move your herd to a new pasture, the old one should be allowed to rest for a few months.

- Picking up manure from the pasture will prevent any form of re-infection in the herd.

- If you have large bales of hay, you may want to keep them in a round feeder so that they do not rot when the rainy season arrives.

- If you notice any swampy areas or low lying areas that can accumulate mud and water, it must be fixed immediately. If the pasture gets wet completely, you must move your livestock to dry land to ensure that they do not stand around in mud.

- The area around any natural source of water must be checked for excessive mud deposits.

- The edges of the water trough should be free from mud deposits. This will, again, force livestock to stand in mud, leading to weakening of the hooves.

- Your livestock should be offered mineral blocks, especially when they are young. For any supplementation, consult your vet first.

- Make sure that there is enough access to fresh and clean water so that they can drink to their heart's content.

- In case you buy any hay for feeding in the winter months, it should be of the best quality possible. It must be stored correctly. Any hay that seems wet or moldy must be discarded immediately.

Herd management

- New livestock should only be purchased when you are able to find an auction house or local farm that is reputable.

- Make sure that the pig that you buy looks healthy. You must also insist on getting the health history that includes details like worming history and vaccinations.

- When you transport the animal, find the shortest routes possible. This is one of the biggest stressors for your mini.

- When you have a new pig in your home, isolate him from the rest of the herd if you have one.

- Animals that are sick and weak should not be bred.

- If your animal is sick or injured, make sure that you call the vet promptly.

The better the husbandry practices that you follow, the more will it benefit your pig. Observing the behavior of your pet can also come very handy in preventing the escalation of a condition and ensuring that timely aid is provided.

5. First aid

There are a lot of simple measures that you can take to provide immediate care in case of injuries and emergencies. Knowing how you can care for your miniature pig is the first step to being a good owner. In some cases, it may be too late before the vet arrives or you take your pig to the vet.

Injuries in animals never take place in a location or time that is convenient. If you are able to take care of the injury immediately with appropriate care, you can reduce the impact of any injury.

There are a few simple principles that you can apply in each scenario with your pet. Being prepared is to have all the knowledge that is needed along with the right first aid kit. Make sure you consult your vet and learn more skills to take care of your pet.

When the animal is injured, the behavior will be very different from normal. They may not be as calm and docile as you expect them to be, so be careful when you handle an injured animal.

The first thing that you need to do is restrain the animal using a harness. When your pig is restrained properly, it will prevent further injuries to the animal and will also keep you safe.

Here are some of the common issues that you must watch out for:

Cuts, puncture wounds and scrapes

- Wash the wound with a gentle cleanser, running water or saline solution.

- If there is any debris or dirt in the wound, use a lot of saline to flush it out of the wound.

- It helps to use a large syringe or bore needle to wash the area so that you can clean the specific area.

- Even the eyewash that you use with contacts can be used to wash wounds. You can get a large container of this if needed.

- Cover the wound with some water soluble ointments and also antiseptics.

- With water soluble ointments, you will have faster results in comparison to sprays that will make the tissue dry.

- On superficial wounds, you can use an ointment that is petroleum jelly based. These ointments are not recommended when they have a certain chemical composition.

Eye injuries

- If there is any foreign object lodged in the eye it can be washed out with saline that is maintained at body temperature.

- In case you are unable to restrain a pig with eye injuries, your vet may have to tranquilize him before you do anything.

- The eyes are extremely delicate and you must make sure that you do not treat the injury unless you have adequate experience.

- In case of head and eye injuries, you and the animal can be injured severely without necessary precautions.

Bleeding

- Any form of bleeding can be controlled if you can hold the area down with gauze sponges.

- Make sure that the gauze is kept in place while you bandage it snugly enough to clot the blood but not so tight that it would restrict blood flow.

- If you are unable to control blood flow with this technique, you must call your vet immediately. This may require surgical correction.

- You can use blood stopper powder only on superficial wounds. However, these products should never be used on deep wounds.

- If deep wounds are not treated properly, there can be tissue damage, scarring or the formation of abscesses.

Hoof care

- The hood of your pig will present several special challenges.

- Any wound in the hoof must be flushed out immediately.

- For most hoof injuries, it is best to just wash the hoof and the house the animal in a dry environment.

- An absorbent wrap can be used to cover the wound. Many farms use disposable diapers as effective covers for these wounds. If not, you can even use cotton.

- If you are using an elastic wrap, make sure that it is not too tight, restricting the flow of blood.

Bloating and frothy bloat

- This is common in ruminants.

- It is usually caused when the forage consists of an excessive amount of succulent legumes.

- You can use commercial products like BloatGuard to break the froth down. Vegetable oil can be used in a small quantity as a reliable home remedy.

- If the animal has free gas bloat, a speculum with a garden hose is normally used.

- In extreme cases, the vet will use a bloat trochar.

Handy first aid kit for your pig

Having the right tools and equipment in place can be a life saver in case of an emergency. When you have a miniature pig in your home, you can make a first aid kit on your own with the following items:

- Heavy duty scissors

- Flashlight

- Needle nosed plier

- Halter and rope

- Wire cutters

- Disposable gloves

- Skin cleanser

- Gauze sponges

- Sterile saline solution

- Water soluble ointment

- Frothy bloat equipment

- Medical tape or duct tape

- Fly repellant

- Large syringes

- Antibiotic eye ointment

- Thermometer

- Rolled cotton

- Calcium gel or calcium borogluconate

- Mineral oil

- A small dose of epinephrine

- Hoof nippers

- A knife

- A small container

- Water based lubricant

- Phone numbers of your vet, state vet and any emergency facility

It is recommended that you have your pig checked by your vet on a regular basis. It is true that medical expenses for your pig can be high. That is an important factor to keep in mind. You can also speak with insurance companies to help you find a plan that can cover your pig in case of any major procedures.

Chapter 8: Grooming the micro pig

When you decide to keep a micro pig as a pet, you should understand that you will have to pay attention to the basic cleaning and grooming of the micro pig. This is essential to keep the micro pig clean and healthy. Not only will your micro pig appear neat and clean, he will also be saved from many unwanted diseases.

When you are looking at grooming sessions for your micro pig, you should pay special attention to the micro pig's ears, nails, teeth and its bathing. This chapter will help you to understand the various dos and don'ts while grooming your pet micro pig.

Sanitation is the key to good husbandry. You need to ensure that your pet is clean and well-groomed. Miniature pigs tend to have an unpleasant odor when they are cleaned regularly.

1. Bathing your pig

A good bath is needed to make sure that there is no dirt or manure on your pig's body. Of course, this needs to be done carefully to prevent startling the animal, leading to unpleasant situations. A regular bath can prevent possible infections on the skin and also the chances of any parasites affecting the health of the anima.

Here are a few steps that will help you keep your pig clean in the most effortless way:

If you do not have access to warm water to bathe your pig with, make sure that you wait for a warm day to carry this out. Pigs tend to be very unpleasant when they are washed in cold conditions. They will display bad behavior all day long.

The first thing you need to do is secure the pig using a rope or a halter that is fastened to a collar. The best option is to tie your mini to the side of a wall or the building. Using a pole to fasten the pig will lead to him walking around in circles. The rope that you choose should not be more than 1.5 feet in length. That way, your pig can eat some grass or hay when you are bathing her, but will not get too much room to move around. A shorter rope is recommended if this is the first bath you are giving your pig or if he is known to misbehave during a bath.

The knot that you use to secure the animal should be easy to release. That way, in case of a tangle or a fall, you can release the pig safely.

Wet the whole body of the pig starting from the legs and then working your way up to the back. Make sure that you are cautious in the beginning, as the reaction of the pig to water is unpredictable. The area around the head and face should be cleaned in the end to make sure that you do not get any soap or water in the ears and eyes.

It is common for pigs to have mud or manure stuck in their hair. You will face this issue more often with long haired minis. If there are large chunks you may have to carefully cut it out without making the coat seem different.

If you have a pressure washer, it will come in quite handy when it comes to removing dirt from the tail or the legs. The water acts like a comb to remove this dirt from the hair. Make sure that the power washer does not hurt your pig. This means that it should not be used on sensitive areas like the face, belly and the udder.

You need to use soap on your pig to get him fully clean. Soap up one side at a time. Then you can move to the feet and the legs. The best option is baby shampoo. You can also consult your vet to provide special soap that can improve the condition of the hair and the skin. Using your hand is good enough for most areas. A hard brush is needed on the legs and the back to remove any dirt.

The soap must be rinsed off fully. To do this, start at the backline and then move down to the legs. Make sure that you do not leave any soap on the body, as the chemicals can cause skin problems.

Don't let the pig into the housing area. Let her walk around in the sun and dry off fully. You do not want hay and other material sticking to the wet hair, making your efforts go in vain.

Be patient with the pig. If there is a lot of squirming, allow him to settle down before you wash him. If you have a large pond that you can lure him, into, it is the easiest option to give him a nice and clean bath.

2. Hoof trimming

Lameness in pigs is a very common issue. There are several factors that contribute and may be interrelated in some cases, but one of the main reasons why pigs have hoof related issues is when the hoof is uneven. That leads to imbalanced weight on the legs, causing issues with the one that is carrying most of the weight.

If one claw is being overloaded, it will become sensitive, prone to lameness and very unstable. Make sure that you check the hooves of your pig regularly and trim them for two reasons:

- In order to restore the weight balance on all four claws equally.

- To check for any possible lesions on the hooves.

You need to examine the pig and make sure that trimming is required. If you over-trim you can put the pig at risk of walking issues.

There are four steps in a good claw trimming process. Make sure that every foot is approached with this technique. This will avoid over trimming. It is recommended that you seek the assistance of someone with experience before you try to do this on your own.

Step 1: Measuring toe length

- The measurement will begin at the hairline to the tip of the toe. This is called the front wall. You will measure the inside claw present on the hind feet.

- If the claw length is more than 3 inches, it should be removed. You will make a cut that is perpendicular to the sole. When you do so, the toe will have a square end.

- The inside claw on the hind feet must be trimmed foot. Then proceed to the other claws to make sure that they match. This is the same process with the front legs but you will start from the outer claw.

Step 2: Maintain the thickness of the sole

- The thickness of the sole at the toe and the length of the claw are directly correlated. The thickness of the sole will be measured from the tip of the toe that you just cut. If the thickness is more than 0.25 inches, you can reduce the thickness.

- When you trim the sole, start from the front and move to the back. The horn on the hind claw should not be removed. The sole thickness should be maintained at 0.25 inches from the tip of the toe.

- The claws that are less than 3 inches should not be trimmed. You must also never trim any hoof with a sole thickness that is less than 0.25 inches.

- In most cases you will only have to trim the outside of your rear claw. That way you will be able restore balance and remove overgrowth if any.

- When you apply pressure on the sole, it should not seem flexible after trimming.

Step 3: Measure the depth of the heel

- You can measure the depth of the heel from the bottom of the sole to just below the hairline. This measurement should be taken on the outside of the claw or the heel wall juncture.

- If you see that the measurement is more than 1.5 inches, you should trim the horn from that heel.

- Usually, heel depth is low in pigs that are housed in an area with a concrete floor.

Step 4: Maintain claw and heel balance

- The surface between the inner and outer surface should be flat and capable of bearing weight after you are done with the trimming process.

- The sole will not be trimmed if you feel that it flexes when you apply pressure with your thumb or finger.

- The heel and claw balance should be checked. For this, you can use the front walls of both legs and place them on a flat surface that will go across both heels and both the toes. It should also be measured from the toe to the heel on both feet. If you can see some light from below the flat surface, it means that you have to check the trim that you have made.

You will get a special hoof trimmer in any pet store. You can also order online or buy one from the vet. These trimmers are very similar to the nail file that we use in our homes to remove any excess growth.

If you feel confident, you can go through with this. However, during your first attempt, you can have someone with experience accompany you. You may even seek the assistance of your vet if you feel like it is a difficult task for you.

When trimmed improperly, the pig struggles to gain balance when walking or just standing. If you over trim, the animal may feel a lot of pain is also susceptible to several injuries. Make sure that you have a step by step approach that allows the animal to calm down fully before you try to trim the hoof.

Chapter 9: Training the micro pig

It is very important to train the animal to make him more suitable to a household. By nature, micro pigs can be a little naughty. You will have to train them to tame them.

Like training most other animals, micro pig training will also require you to be patient. You will have to do a few trial and errors before you can be sure that your micro pig is well trained. You should remember to have fun even during the training phase.

The training phase can be a great opportunity for you to learn more about your little pet. No matter how much you read about a micro pig, your pet will have some individual properties that will separate him from the rest of the lot. This is a good time to learn about all these properties.

The more you learn about your pet, the stronger the bond you form with him. You should remember to not take the training phase as a cumbersome thing. In fact, take it as an opportunity to form an everlasting bond with your pet. Your pet will also understand you better during this time.

While you have to be regular during this phase, you should not be harsh and rude. Don't beat the micro pig and terrorize it. You will only scare the pet and jeopardize your relationship with him. If you have your doubts, it is better to read more about them and then make your decisions regarding the micro pig's training phase.

1. Training your mini pig

While not many people think of pigs, regular or miniature, as pets, the truth is that they can be a lot of fun to be around. Miniature pigs are very playful and their small size also makes them more approachable.

Now that you have learnt all about approaching the pig correctly, the next step is to train them. Pigs and piglets can be trained for shows and also to run errands on your farm. This training practice makes the bond between the owner and the pig a lot stronger, as it has the potential to build a lot of trust.

Halter training

This is a very important type of training if you want to present your miniature pig or piglet in livestock shows. Also known as halter breaking, this process is time consuming and requires a lot of patience and persistence from your end. Irrespective of the breed that you have, it is best that you start this training when the pig is very young.

The advantage is that you will be able to handle a piglet better than an adult, who is much stronger. Halter training a pig is very similar to a horse. Of course, the behavior of the two animals is quite different, which means that you have to change your approach quite a bit.

When you are halter training livestock, the methods differ based on the age and the size of the animal. It is easier to get a piglet on a halter and lead him around for a while. In the case of older animals, they will take some time to get used to the halter and will also need to understand what you really expect from them.

Typically, a piglet that has been weaned from the mother recently is the easiest to halter train.

The technique mentioned in this section is effective on the younger piglets and the older ones. The method itself was devised for livestock that are still not of the weaning age, that is, about 6 months of age. However, it works equally well on livestock of all breeds and ages.

Catching the piglet

The first step is to get hold of the piglet that you want to train. Leading them into a smaller enclosure is a good idea, as they will not have too much space to run away from you.

If the piglet is just a few days old, they tend to be a little dopey. That means that you can lead the piglet to a corner and then get hold of him. The mother should not be around, especially if she is not halter trained herself. She will show you signs of discomfort when you begin to corner the piglet and try to get a lasso around the neck so that you can lead them to halter training.

When they are older than a week, it is harder to catch the piglet. However, if you learn how to approach them calmly without startling them, you will be able to get a lasso around the neck quite easily. Using this lasso, you can lead the piglet to the part of the farm where you wish to have the halter on him.

That said, be prepared for a lot of resistance when you try to pull a piglet by the neck using a lasso. They will try to break free as quickly as possible and will put up quite the fight. Wait for the piglet to settle down and take a few steps forward. Do this until he is walking comfortably with you.

Now if your piglets have been bottle fed, they are most likely used to the presence of human beings. In that case, the protest will be absent and you will also find it very easy to catch the piglet. All you have to do is present the bottle that you feed him from and he will walk towards you voluntarily.

Getting the halter on

When you have successfully lead the piglet to the area that you want to halter him in, you can begin to do so while you keep a strong grip on the rope that you used to lead him.

The halter will go over the head and the ears first before going over the nose. The ears should be looped through the halter to make it fit comfortably. A rope halter will have an adjustable portion that will go on the nose. You will keep it as wide open as possible when you get the nose of the livestock into it. Then, you can tighten the rope around the muzzle.

You also have the option of using a leather halter that will go on the same way as a rope halter. Make sure that the head piece is snug but not so tight that it pinches the muzzle. Use a non-show halter to begin with.

If the piglet has been unruly in the past or if you are dealing with an older pig, having a head gate installed is a good idea. That way, there is no chance of the piglet running away when you are just half way through getting the halter on. You also will be able to prevent any injury to yourself if the piglet or older pig is unhappy with the halter and reacts in a negative manner.

Following this you can connect the lead onto the metal ring that is present on a leather halter. With a rope halter, you do not have to add a lead, as it already comes with a rope that is attached to the halter. Once this is done, the halter should be left on for a few days, preferably a week. That way, the piglet gets used to the halter and will also understand the amount of pressure that is applied on the halter in case he accidentally steps on it. You will move on to the next step only when the piglet is comfortable with the halter.

Stay close to the piglet

This should be done especially if you are not bottle feeding the pig. That will help him get used to your presence. You can give him range cubes and other treats when you are around. Hand feeding is recommended, as that will encourage the piglet to approach you comfortably. If your piglet is not particularly fond of range cubes, you can even offer some grain from your hand. The goal is to get him to approach you rather than you having to corner him or chase him around to catch him.

Keep the housing area of the piglet extremely clean and make sure that he is not in a crowded area in the resting area. The lesser the stress, the better the response to halter training. You must also talk to him in a calm voice at all times.

The next step is to practice tying the piglet using the halter lead. Make a few loops of the lead around a post and then tie a knot. That will keep it sturdy and will prevent the piglet from breaking loose. The distance between the post and the head of the piglet should not be more than 12 inches.

The first time you tie the piglet, keep him there for not more than 30 minutes. As he gets used to it, you may increase the time being tied. When the piglet is tied up, stroke his chin or ears to make him feel relaxed. This will also lead to positive associations with you in the future.

Using the lead

The next step from there is to actually get the piglet to walk on a lead. Hold the lead in your hand and keep it short in length. Slowly walk forward and encourage the piglet to do the same.

You must stay on the left side of the piglet. Never allow the piglet to lead. You must stay ahead. If the piglet tries to step ahead of you, just stop, collect the piglet and start only after he is beside you.

Never drag the piglet along as you walk. Pull gently and encourage the piglet to walk. When he begins to walk, just release the lead a little. You will do this until the piglet learns to walk next to you. It may take several attempts, so be patient.

Then, you can start turning when you are walking the piglet on the lead. You have to watch out for any signs of protests such as jumping or pulling back. If this happens, calm down, get the piglet beside you and then continue with the training. Try not to let go and keep a strong grip on the lead.

In the event that the piglet escapes, catch him calmly using the methods mentioned above. Once that is done, you will continue to train. The training session will always end on your terms. If not, he will pick up bad habits like pulling. The more you practice, the better you will get at leading the pig using a halter.

2. Training pigs to pull

Pigs make great draft animals and have always been used to pull loads across farms. The fact that they are extremely strong makes it easy for them to pull an item with a few farmland items on it.

However, the other thing to keep in mind is that they are easily spooked by an object following them around. That is why training them gradually to get used to the cart is necessary and requires you to take one step at a time.

Unless your pig is used to being lead with a halter, he is not ready to pull. When you are able to lead the pig without much protest, it will be easy to get them used to a cart.

Now, like any other training that you provide, the earlier you begin, the faster the results are going to be. It is also much easier to handle a piglet. However, since you are working with miniature pigs, you should be able to handle them comfortably even when they are adults.

With minis, you should avoid heavy farm work on a large piece of land. This work is typically carried out by stronger and more robust animals like oxen. With minis, you can get them to pull small weights across a short distance. Each breed has a different draft power. You can talk to your vet about this and decide how much volume of work your mini will be able to handle.

Traditionally, livestock that originate from upland areas have better pulling ability and are considered to be ideal draft animals. One of the best documents about the draft strength of each breed is available with the German Agricultural Society.

To begin with you can put a horse collar around the neck of the pig. Using an open collar is a good idea, as the head of the pig is much larger. The horse collar will be used upside down, as the head of the pig is designed opposite to that of a horse with the sensitive part around the neck.

You will notice that the trace hooks are higher on the neck. This is alright as the pig must be drawn higher. If the pig seems comfortable then you can move on. If not, leave the drafting gear on for a while and just practice putting it on for a few days.

3. How to make the pig cooperate

There is a step by step approach to making sure that your pig is cooperative throughout the process. This takes some practice and dedication from your end.

You need to have a separate enclosure that is clean and sanitized for milking. The goal is to have the pig trot in comfortably when you open the door.

Keep the pig tethered

The lesser the movement of the pig, the easier it is. When you tether the pig, here are a few things that you need to do:

- The pig must be tethered such that his head faces a wall. Having a metal ring or a rod on the wall will help you do this easily. A ring is a better option, as it will allow the head to move up and down.

- The lead that you have on the harness is the best option. Tie one end to the ring or rod, keeping the lead short.

- The pig should not be able to move his head from side to side. When the ring moves, he will be able to bend down and reach for the food. The pig will be able to see you from the side and will have an idea about what is going on. That will help him remain calm throughout.

Watch out for kicks

When a pig gets uncomfortable, he will use his back legs to kick the person who is training him. This is not without any warning, however.

The leg will move in a circular motion when the pig is just about to kick. It will go back, circle to the side and then swing forward. Knowing this will help you prepare yourself in case a kick is about to come.

As soon as the back leg moves off the ground, you can say "No!" in a sharp and firm tone to get him to stop the kick.

Conclusion

Thank you again for purchasing this book!

I hope this book was able to help you in understanding the various ways to domesticate and care for micro pigs.

Micro pigs are adorable and lovable animals. These animals have been domesticated for many years. Even though they are loved as pets, they are not very common, and there are still many doubts regarding their domestication methods and techniques. There are many things that the prospective owners don't understand about the animal. They find themselves getting confused as to what should be done and what should be avoided.

A micro pig is a small, naughty animal that will keep you busy and entertained by all its unique antics and mischiefs. It is said that each animal is different from the other. Each one will have some traits that are unique to him. It is important to understand the traits that differentiate the micro pig from other animals. You also have to be sure that you can provide for the animal, so it is important to be acquainted with the dos and don'ts of keeping the micro pig.

If you wish to raise a micro pig as a pet, there are many things that you need to understand before you can domesticate the animal. You need to make sure that you are ready in terms of the right preparation. There are certain unique characteristics of the animal that make him adorable, but these traits can also be very confusing for many people. You can't domesticate the animal with all the confusions in your head.

If you are still contemplating whether you want to domesticate the micro pig or not, then it becomes all the more important for you to understand everything regarding the pet very well. You can only make a wise decision when you are acquainted will all these and more. When you are planning to domesticate a micro pig as a pet, you should lay special emphasis on learning about its behavior, habitat requirements, diet requirements and common health issues.

When you decide to domesticate an animal, it is important that you understand the animal and its species well. It is important to learn the basic nature and mannerisms of the animal. This book will help you to equip yourself with this knowledge. You will be able to appreciate the micro pigs for what they are. You will also know what to expect from the animal. This will help you to decide whether the micro pig is the right choice for you or not. If you already have a micro pig, then this book will help you to strengthen your bond with your pet.

Thank you and good luck!

References

Note: at the time of printing, all the websites below were working. As the internet changes rapidly, some sites might no longer be live when you read this book. That is, of course, out of our control.

http://www.nationalgeographic.com

www.ehow.co.uk

https://en.wikipedia.org

https://www.lovethatpet.com

http://www.micro pig-world.com

https://www.thespruce.com

https://www.bluecross.org.uk

https://pethelpful.com

http://www.drsfostersmith.com

https://www.cuteness.com

http://www.arkive.org

https://www.hillsborovet.com

www.training.ntwc.org

www.wildlifehealth.org

http://animaldiversity.org

https://a-z-animals.com

http://www.marshallpet.com

https://www.all-about-micro pigs.com

Printed in Great Britain
by Amazon

57628295R00068